NAPOLÉON BONAPARTE

Borgo Press Books Edited & Translated by FRANK J. MORLOCK

Alcestis: A Play in Five Acts, by Philippe Quinault * *Anna Karenina: A Play in Five Acts*, by Edmond Guiraud, from Leo Tolstoy * *Anthony: A Play in Five Acts*, by Alexandre Dumas, Père * *Atys: A Play in Five Acts*, by Philippe Quinault * *The Boss Lady: A Play in Five Acts*, by Paul Féval, Père * *The Children of Captain Grant: A Play in Five Acts*, by Jules Verne & Adolphe d'Ennery * *Cleopatra: A Play in Five Acts*, by Victorien Sardou * *Crime and Punishment: A Play in Three Acts*, by Frank J. Morlock, from Fyodor Dostoyevsky * *Don Quixote: A Play in Three Acts*, by Victorien Sardou, from Miguel de Cervantes * *The Dream of a Summer Night: A Fantasy Play in Three Acts*, by Paul Meurice * *Falstaff: A Play in Four Acts*, by William Shakespeare, John Dennis, William Kendrick, & Frank J. Morlock * *The Idiot: A Play in Three Acts*, by Frank J. Morlock, from Fyodor Dostoyevsky * *Isis: A Play in Five Acts*, by Philippe Quinault * *Jesus of Nazareth: A Play in Three Acts*, by Paul Demasy * *The Jew of Venice: A Play in Five Acts*, by Ferdinand Dugué * *Joan of Arc: A Play in Five Acts*, by Charles Desnoyer * *The Lily of the Valley: A Play in Five Acts*, by Théodore Barrière & Arthur de Beauplan, from Honoré de Balzac * *Lord Byron in Venice: A Play in Three Acts*, by Jacques Ancelot * *Louis XIV and the Affair of the Poisons: A Play in Five Acts*, by Victorien Sardou * *The Man Who Saw the Devil: A Play in Two Acts*, by Gaston Leroux * *Mathias Sandorf: A Play in Three Acts*, by Jules Verne & William Busnach * *Michael Strogoff: A Play in Five Acts*, by Jules Verne & Adolphe d'Ennery * *Les Misérables: A Play in Two Acts*, by Victor Hugo, Paul Meurice, & Charles Victor Hugo * *Monte Cristo, Part One: A Play in Five Acts*, by Alexandre Dumas, Père * *Monte Cristo, Part Two: A Play in Five Acts*, by Alexandre Dumas, Père * *Monte Cristo, Part Three: A Play in Five Acts*, by Alexandre Dumas, Père * *Monte Cristo, Part Four: A Play in Five Acts*, by Alexandre Dumas, Père * *The Musketeers: A Play in Five Acts*, by Alexandre Dumas, Père * *The Mysteries of Paris: A Play in Five Acts*, by Eugène Sue & Prosper Dinaux * *Napoléon Bonaparte: A Play in Six Acts*, by Alexandre Dumas, Père * *Ninety-Three: A Play in Four Acts*, by Victor Hugo & Paul Meurice * *Notes from the Underground: A Play in Two Acts*, by Frank J. Morlock, from Fyodor Dostoyevsky * *Outrageous Women: Lady MacBeth and Other French Plays*, edited by Frank J. Morlock * *Peau de Chagrin: A Play in Five Acts*, by Louis Judicis, from Honoré de Balzac * *The Prisoner of the Bastille: A Play in Five Acts*, by Alexandre Dumas, Père * *A Raw Youth: A Play in Five Acts*, by Frank J. Morlock, from Fyodor Dostoyevsky * *Richard Darlington: A Play in Three Acts*, by Alexandre Dumas, Père * *The San Felice: A Play in Five Acts*, by Maurice Drack, from Alexander Dumas, Père * *Saul and David: A Play in Five Acts*, by Voltaire * *Shylock, the Merchant of Venice: A Play in Three Acts*, by Alfred de Vigny * *Socrates: A Play in Three Acts*, by Voltaire * *The Son of Porthos: A Play in Five Acts*, by Émile Blavet, from M. Paul Mahalin * *The Stendhal Hamlet Scenarios and Other Shakespearean Shorts from the French*, edited by Frank J. Morlock * *A Summer Night's Dream: A Play in Three Acts*, by Joseph-Bernard Rosier & Adolphe de Leuwen * *The Three Musketeers: A Play in Five Acts*, by Alexandre Dumas, Père * *Urbain Grandier and the Devils of Loudon: A Play in Four Acts*, by Alexandre Dumas, Père * *The Voyage Through the Impossible: A Play in Three Acts*, by Jules Verne & Adolphe d'Ennery * *The Whites and the Blues: A Play in Five Acts*, by Alexandre Dumas, Père * *William Shakespeare: A Play in Six Acts*, by Ferdinand Dugué

NAPOLÉON BONAPARTE

A PLAY IN SIX ACTS

by

Alexandre Dumas, Père

Translated and Adapted by Frank J. Morlock

THE BORGO PRESS

An Imprint of Wildside Press LLC

MMX

CONTENTS

DEDICATION

To

GERRY TETRAULT

CAST OF CHARACTERS

- Napoléon Bonaparte
- A Spy
- Lorrain
- Junot
- General Cartaux
- Salicetti
- Fréron
- Gasparin
- Albitte
- General Dugommier
- A Sentinel
- Joséphine
- General Duroc
- A Mountebank
- A Public Crier
- A Passerby
- Another Passerby
- A Merchant of Umbrellas
- Charles Bourrienne
- An Usher
- Labredèche
- A Fop/Dandy
- A Child
- General Berthier
- Caulaincourt
- Davout
- Rapp
- Mortier
- Talma
- The Minister of War
- Murat
- The Emperor of Austria
- The King of Saxony
- The King of Württemberg

- The King of Prussia
- 1st Soldier
- 2nd Soldier
- 3rd Soldier
- 4th Soldier
- An Aide de Camp
- A Young Woman
- An Express Messenger
- An Envoy
- Ragusa
- Trévise
- Rustan
- King Louis XVIII (a non-speaking part)
- The Marquis de la Feuillade
- An Usher
- A Solicitor
- An Old Soldier
- The Minister
- The Grand Marshal
- 2nd Usher
- The Marquise
- A Doctor
- The Abbé
- The Little Girl Cousin
- A Valet
- A Ship's Captain
- 1st Gamekeeper
- 2nd Gamekeeper
- A Courtier
- A Gendarme
- A Sailor
- A Sentry
- Sir Hudson Lowe
- Marchand
- Antonmarchi
- Bertrand
- Las Cases
- An English Officer
- Madame Bertrand (and her children)
- People, Merchants, Soldiers, Ladies, Grisettes, Vivandières, etc.

ACT I

Tableau 1

Before Toulon. The interior of a redoubt. From the windows one can see the city under siege, and the chain of rocks which ring the forts.

> *(A sentinel and conscript soldiers sleeping by a tree. AT RISE, three men come to relieve the sentinel; a conscript takes his place.)*

CONSCRIPT

The orders?

SENTINEL

Don't let anyone pass. Watch the road from Toulon to Marseille.

CONSCRIPT

The password?

SENTINEL

Toulon and Liberty.

CONSCRIPT

Good.

> *(the soldiers are leaving)*

Wait! Wait!

(they return)

What did you say?

SENTINEL

Toulon and Liberty.

CONSCRIPT

And I will allow all those who say that to pass?

SENTINEL

Yes.

CONSCRIPT

You can go now.

(he repeats again and again).

Toulon and Liberty. Toulon and Liberty. That's it.

(singing)

It's sad to be a police man.
It's good to be a soldier.
When the drum rolls,
Bye, bye girls.
When the drum rolls,
The nation's moving.

(JUNOT, who rises at the beginning of this song and follows the soldier from behind to the moment he returns.)

JUNOT

Tell me, citizen conscript, what's your name?

CONSCRIPT

I'm called Lorrain, Lorrain, 'cause I come from Lorrain.

JUNOT

Well, Citizen Lorrain, then you will make a tour of this camp.

CONSCRIPT

What's that, sergeant?

JUNOT

Because one doesn't sing under arms.

(goes off)

CONSCRIPT

That's so! Next time, I will remember. He's a real good kid, the sergeant. He could have sent me to the stockade. Best be consoled.

(Enter BONAPARTE with JUNOT)

BONAPARTE

And you tell me there are not enough artillery men who wish to serve in my battery?

JUNOT

Fort Mulgrove is only 125 yards away and during the last attack, seventy artillery men were killed out of eighty.

(A bullet passes and strikes the branch of a tree which falls at the feet of Bonaparte.)

BONAPARTE

We must appeal for volunteers.

JUNOT

I have done it and not one has offered.

BONAPARTE

Ah, it's like that! Sergeant, write on this paper in large letters. "Battery of Fearless Men."

(A bullet tears up some of the embankment and sprays the Sergeant, who is writing.)

JUNOT

Good.

(shaking his paper)

I won't need any sand to dry it.

BONAPARTE

What's your name?

JUNOT

Junot.

BONAPARTE

I won't forget it.

LORRAIN

Who goes there?

JUNOT

Imbecile. You see quite well it's the General in Chief and the representatives of the people.

BONAPARTE

(to Sergeant Junot)

Put this sign in front of the battery, and everybody will want to be there.

CARTAUX

Citizen Commandant, we have received a plan of attack from Paris and we've come to communicate it to you.

BONAPARTE

And who is the author of this plan?

CARTAUX

The celebrated general D'Acron.

BONAPARTE

Who perhaps has never seen the city. It's the fifth plan they've sent from Paris and the worst of my artillerymen can do no worse than the best of them all. Let's see the plan.

CARTAUX

(reading)

General Cartaux seizes all the positions occupied by the enemy by land and will abandon entirely the sea. He will conquer, whatever the price may be, the Forts Parson, Saint Antoine, Lastigues, St. Catherine, and Lamalgue. Once master of these forts, he will proceed without relaxation to the bombardment of the city.

BONAPARTE

And how many men as reinforcements does he send us to execute this plan?

CARTAUX

Not one. We must be content with what we have.

BONAPARTE

Sixty thousand men will not be enough. And with the reinforcements come from the Lyons army, we will hardly have thirty thousand.

FRÉRON

You must still execute the orders of the committee as best you can or your head, citizen general, will answer for the success.

BONAPARTE

(taking his hand)

Citizen Representative, do you see here this citadel encrusted like an eagle's nest between the flanks of this mountain? That's Fort Faron which your committee has ordered us to take. If you want me to execute these orders, find me soldiers who have wings or bring me flying horses to get them there.

GASPARIN

Well, let's restrict ourselves to taking of Fort Lamalgue.

BONAPARTE

Yes, and to get there you will pass your 30,000 men between the first of four forts and the armed-fortified camp before Toulon, and when you have lost half of your men, with the rest, you will attack Fort Lamalgue, constructed by Vauban with his angles opposed to angles, its battery of sixty pieces of artillery and its three thousand-man garrison.

CARTAUX

Citizen Commandant, have you directed a battery of four shrapnel on the powder works?

BONAPARTE

Yes.

CARTAUX

Well?

BONAPARTE

I threw twenty Howitzers' Shrapnel—of which seventeen have hit.

CARTAUX

Without result?

BONAPARTE

Without result.

CARTAUX

We must continue.

BONAPARTE

Useless.

CARTAUX

Why?

BONAPARTE

The powder has been taken into the city.

FRÉRON

Then we must bombard the city, and profiting from the explosion of a magazine where they stored it—make an attack.

BONAPARTE

Yes, that will be fine, but who will tell me which of the eight hundred houses of Toulon must be burned?

FRÉRON

Burn them all.

BONAPARTE

Must I, a Corsican, tell you that Toulon is French?

SALICETTI

What's the difference! Turenne burned the Palatinate.

BONAPARTE

That was necessary for his plans—here's it's a useless crime.

FRÉRON

Would you be an aristocrat by chance?

(Bonaparte shrugs his shoulders)

Citizen General, we must put an end to this. Attack the city however you wish, but in eight days, the city must be taken—or in nine days I will send you to Paris as a suspect—and in fifteen days—you understand.

CARTAUX

Yes, yes, well then, I will stick by the plan of the committee—the general attack will begin tomorrow.

BONAPARTE

You will lose and you will lose the army with you.

CARTAUX

But what to do then?

(Bonaparte gets up and points to the fort of Little Gibraltar on the map.)

BONAPARTE

There's Toulon.

CARTAUX

There? But not at all. He's showing us the exit from the road-stead. Toulon is not on that side.

(aside)

To take little Gibraltar for Toulon!

BONAPARTE

(forcefully)

There is Toulon, I tell you. Take this fort today and tomorrow or the day after we will enter into Toulon.

SALICETTI

It's the best-defended.

BONAPARTE

Proof that it is the most important.

GASPARIN

The British commandant himself has judged it to be impregnable—he said that if we carry it, he'll become a Jacobin.

BONAPARTE

Let me lead the attack and in twelve hours, I will take it myself or my sword in my own breast.

SALICETTI

But we will lose 10,000 men.

BONAPARTE

Ten thousand, twenty thousand, provided I still have 3,000 to put in garrison.

FRÉRON

Ah, there's the philanthropist who doesn't want to burn 800 houses and wants to kill 10,000 men.

BONAPARTE

(walking away)

Simpleton!

CARTAUX

All right then, Citizen Commandant, be ready to bombard the city.

BONAPARTE

From here?

CARTAUX

Yes—during this time.

BONAPARTE

There are two projectiles per cannon.

CARTAUX

No—you can get more.

BONAPARTE

Cannoneers—commence fire.

(The cannoneers command all the length of the line. Bonaparte points a cannon himself, takes a match, puts fire to the piece and returns without looking where the shot landed.)

CARTAUX

(who's watching attentively)

He's right. The shell landed two hundred meters at least from the outer works.

FRÉRON

Never mind! This young man annoys me. He acts like an aristocrat, but we will make him obey.

GASPARIN

Citizens, the commandant appears to know what he must do better than anyone, let him manage—

FRÉRON

(without listening to Gasparin, to Cartaux)

General, come give your orders and then in an hour, we will commence the attack.

(Bonaparte follows him with eyes full of compassion, Cartaux leaves with Salicetti, Gasparin, Fréron, etc.)

BONAPARTE

When will they stop sending us doctors and politicians to command us? It's useless to tell them how to take Toulon.

LORRAIN

(to a peasant who seeks to slide by—without being seen)

Who goes there? Who goes there?

PEASANT

(with a very pronounced provincial accent)

What must I say?

LORRAIN

Eh, well, reply, "Citizen Peasant," for God's sake.

PEASANT

Citizen Peasant.

LORRAIN

That's better. And now go back from where you came. No one can pass.

PEASANT

(without accent)

No one can pass?

BONAPARTE

(starting at the change of voice)

Right—here you can pass.

PEASANT

Thank you, my officer.

BONAPARTE

Listen then.

PEASANT

(aside)

What's he want from me?

BONAPARTE

You are from this country?

PEASANT

Yes, from Ollioules.

BONAPARTE

Ah—and by what chance do you find yourself on this side?

PEASANT

It's those lazy English who requisitioned me by force. To Toulon to work on the fortifications of Fort Malbousquet.

BONAPARTE

And they've sent you back.

PEASANT

No—I've escaped.

BONAPARTE

Why?

PEASANT

There was too much work and not enough money.

BONAPARTE

And you're going?

PEASANT

To Marseille.

BONAPARTE

(shaking his hand)

Bon voyage.

PEASANT

(giving his hand)

Thank you, citizen.

BONAPARTE

What kind of work did you do?

PEASANT

I dig trenches.

BONAPARTE

And you wear gloves to work?

PEASANT

(aside)

The devil?

(aloud)

Why?

BONAPARTE

Yes, if you hadn't taken this precaution the sun and fatigue would burn and harden the hands. See, I who pride myself on having white and beautiful hands. A peasant who has worked how many days?

PEASANT

Fifteen.

BONAPARTE

Fifteen days at the fortifications—also white and also pretty like mine. What a fool I am.

(to one or two around him).

He's a spy!

PEASANT

(frightened)

Me?

BONAPARTE

You know English?

PEASANT

(aside)

Imbecile!

BONAPARTE

Ah, it's not surprising—you stayed fifteen days with the redcoats and you have had time to learn their language.

PEASANT

I know a few words.

BONAPARTE

Enough to read the address on a letter that they told you to carry, right?

PEASANT

Me, to whom?

BONAPARTE

Eh—how would I know? To some former aristocrat, without doubt, to announce to him that Louis XVIII has been proclaimed in Toulon.

PEASANT

Devil of a man! Ah, if you believe that, you need only search me.

BONAPARTE

No—it will suffice that you give me what you have in your pocket.

PEASANT

(withdrawing stuff from his pocket and giving it slowly)

Here's a flint and a Spanish knife.

BONAPARTE

Yes—which can at need be used as a dagger.

PEASANT

And a notebook which is not elegant, but then we are not dandies. Look in my pockets—if you wish, Citizen Commandant, I have no secrets, not I.

BONAPARTE

(examining the papers)

And I, I am not curious.

(holding up a page, lighter than the others)

Were you afraid of running out of paper that made you add this sheet?

PEASANT

This sheet?

BONAPARTE

Yes—you see that it is neither the same grain nor the same color. Lend me this knife.

PEASANT

My word, I didn't pay so much attention. All I know is that it is blank paper—if you wish to write on it.

BONAPARTE

That is my intention. But it is damp and we must dry it first.

PEASANT

At the fire.

BONAPARTE

Yes—and taking care not to burn it. Cannoneer, a match.

PEASANT

(aside)

Heaven and earth.

(looking around him, he sees that only the sentinel prevents his escape. He withdraws a pistol from his pocket, rushes toward the sentinel, fires and wounds Lorrain in the arm, but Lorrain seizes him after a wrestling match.)

BONAPARTE

(shouting)

Arrest the spy from the English and the émigrés.

(soldiers throw themselves on the spy. Lorrain who never let go, brings him back).

Now cannoneer, bring a match.

(to the spy)

Well, what do you say? Isn't it a marvel how this paper is covered with writing, signed by General in Chief, Hood. "To Monsieur, brother of the King."

SPY

I am lost.

BONAPARTE

Wretch.

PEASANT

Stupid, yes. Wretch, no.

BONAPARTE

(with scorn).

A spy!

SPY

Well, the English gave me parole to be a spy and I have served them loyally. You were more clever than I, that's all.

(turning)

Sergeant—nine-man squad.

BONAPARTE

What?

SPY

Well, yes. The trial of a spy consists of two words. Aim and Fire. The procedure is quickly finished.

BONAPARTE

What a strange place for courage to hide.

SPY

Ah, you are proud of yourself, you. Vain talent! The courage of a soldier! It takes the noise of the instruments of war and the smell of powder to excite such courage, and to say: "the fatherland" as you die. True courage—which is mine, is that of a man who obscurely risks twenty times a day a life that he can lose only in an ignoble way, to which men attach the word shameful, an infamous death, like the death of a forger or a murderer.

BONAPARTE

And what are you then?

SPY

I am a man that no prejudice can stop, that no danger can frighten, who plays slowly with death, who, if a great man had understood me, would attach me to him, body and soul like a familiar demon, who—

(A sergeant entering with nine armed soldiers.)

SERGEANT

Who's to be shot?

SPY

I am. Who, I say, can dress in all costumes, borrow all manners speak all languages. To him I would render, in life or death service, a thousand times the value of the gold he'd given me. Here I am now; a spy, a species of thinking animal, a variety of man who's heart beats, whose voice speaks, who can save an empire, perhaps—and who in ten minutes will be a corpse with eight balls in his body and only good for throwing to the fish in the estuary. Do you understand, that's what I am?

BONAPARTE

Have you something to ask of me?

SPY

Oh, you soldiers. When you are where I am, you will ask that they don't blindfold you and that you give the command to fire yourself. You are privileged in everything. No, I cannot ask that, I demand only that you don't make me wait.

BONAPARTE

I give you five minutes. You can employ them to tell the Sergeant your last wishes. Perhaps you have a wife, children, a mother—

SPY

Nothing.

(Bonaparte sits musing and writes)

Sergeant, here in the handle of this knife is a bill of twenty-five pounds sterling. That's a little more than 600 francs, payable in gold, you see, not in miserable paper money. Take it, and give it to your men if I fall without a twitch. If they don't kill me quick, it's for you. Where's the handkerchief?

SERGEANT

Here.

SPY

Give it to me.

(The Sergeant leads him, conducts him center stage.)

SERGEANT

On your knees.

SPY

(raising his blindfold)

Let me see the sky one more time. Good. I'm ready.

(At the first roll of the drum, the soldiers line up, at the second roll, they ready their arms, at the third, they aim.)

BONAPARTE

(rising and in a strong voice)

Post arms!

(gestures with his hand)

Go.

(The soldiers leave, Bonaparte goes to the spy, and tears off the blindfold)

Come here. Your death is useless to me. I have need of your life. You are brave—well, what's the matter?

SPY

Nothing—wait. A dizziness. My knees are giving way—let me sit.

BONAPARTE

You are brave. With a word, your life touched eternity. I didn't pronounce that word. You owe me then the days that remain to you, the heaven that you see, the air that you breathe. All this belongs to me. Do you consecrate all this to me?

SPY

Eternally!

(rising with solemnity)

And I will be your valet, your dog, your spy, even. They only gave me money, you, you have given me my life.

BONAPARTE

I believe you. Listen and come here.

SPY

An instant. I will be only for you; I will belong to no one except you? You will neither give me away nor sell me?

BONAPARTE

No.

SPY

If you do either, I become free at that instant.

BONAPARTE

I authorize you to.

SPY

That's fine. Speak.

BONAPARTE

You are allowed by General Hood to go back to Toulon?

SPY

I can enter and leave at any time.

BONAPARTE

In what part of the city have they moved the powder that was in this bastion?

SPY

In the basement of a house in the Rue St. Roch, the Rock, as it is called.

BONAPARTE

Well, go back right now. It would only take a grenade to explode those powders.

SPY

Exactly.

BONAPARTE

You will await my signal. A bomb dropped from here will give it to you—Toulon will awaken with a start as the earth trembles; its garrison will have to contain the people and quench the fire. Meanwhile, I will take Little Gibraltar, which is the key to Toulon. You understand?

SPY

Yes.

BONAPARTE

You are decided?

SPY

(getting ready to leave)

I am going.

(returning)

The password.

BONAPARTE

(hesitating)

The password.

SPY

Don't say it, if you wish, Citizen Commandant, but they will fire on me, they will probably kill me—and then, who will return to the city and who will set off the powder?

BONAPARTE

You're right. Besides, I don't intend to confide in you by half—Toulon and Liberty.

(The spy waves and goes rapidly.)

SENTINEL

No one passes.

SPY

(half voice)

Toulon and Liberty.

(Exit the spy.)

(Enter Gasparin.)

BONAPARTE

Here's another representative of the people.

GASPARIN

I was looking for you.

BONAPARTE

Here I am.

GASPARIN

Do you know, you appear to me to be the only one who understands something about a siege.

BONAPARTE

Do you speak as you think?

GASPARIN

Yes.

BONAPARTE

Well, you're right, Citizen Representative.

GASPARIN

If I were in charge, I'd order you to direct the whole business. I've asked them to do that, but the general in chief and my two colleagues are opposed to it. They hold to their plan of attack.

BONAPARTE

They're wrong.

GASPARIN

Listen. Six days ago, I wrote to the committee. I am asking for Cartaux to be replaced by Dugommier.

BONAPARTE

About time! With him, we can talk.

GASPARIN

I await him momentarily. But they have decided to attack forts Faron and Lastigues tonight.

BONAPARTE

We will be wiped out.

GASPARIN

Do you dare to take on yourself a great responsibility?

BONAPARTE

I don't know.

GASPARIN

You command the artillery. See to it not one piece of artillery leaves this battery. Gain time. Dugommier will arrive and your plan will be adopted. I believe it's good. If it succeeds, you will be Brigadier, if it fails, your head will fall on the scaffold.

BONAPARTE

Not one piece of artillery will budge from its place and I take that on myself.

GASPARIN

But will your men obey you?

BONAPARTE

You see this battery? Since it was set up here two hundred artillery men have been killed by their cannons. No one wants to serve here. An hour ago, I put up this sign.

(pointing to sign "Battery of Fearless Men")

Junot!

BONAPARTE

JUNOT

(advancing)

Citizen Commandant?

BONAPARTE

How many men are ready to set their names for this battery?

JUNOT

About four hundred.

BONAPARTE

You see if one can count on these man!

GASPARIN

Especially if commanded by you. Goodbye, and don't forget, I am the first to recognize your military genius.

BONAPARTE

Your name?

GASPARIN

Gasparin.

BONAPARTE

I won't forget it, even on my death bed.

GASPARIN

Adieu, and long live the Republic!

BONAPARTE

Long live the Republic—adieu!

(after he has gone)

Junot, have you received any education?

JUNOT

Not much, my commandant, I know how to write, read, and do a little mathematics. As for Latin and Greek....

BONAPARTE

That's useless for reading Vauban, Folard, and Montecuculli. We have a good translation of Polybius and *Caesar's Commentaries.* That's all you need.

JUNOT

As for my family....

BONAPARTE

I never ask about that. I ask you: are you a good Frenchman with me? That's all.

JUNOT

Yes, my commandant.

BONAPARTE

I don't know if I will become something more than a commander of artillery—in case I do—would you like to be my secretary?

JUNOT

I would like it indeed.

BONAPARTE

Then go tell Muiron, who is your captain, I believe, that I ask you from him. Then return.

(Junot leaves)

(The representatives of the people, Albitti and Fréron, give orders to the cannoneers who are at their cannons.)

BONAPARTE

(who hears this noise)

Who's meddling with my artillery?

ALBITTI

We need some, and we need to take them where we need them.

BONAPARTE

Citizen Representatives—these pieces will not budge from base—cannoneers, to your batteries.

(The cannoneers take their pieces from the representatives and replace them.)

FRÉRON

You disobey our orders?

BONAPARTE

Do your job of representing the people and let me do mine of handling the artillery.

FRÉRON

But...!

BONAPARTE

One more time, these artillery pieces will not budge from here. I'd rather spike them first. Besides, this battery is where it must be. I'll answer with my head.

FRÉRON

Kid, you risk it in disobeying orders of the representatives of the people.

BONAPARTE

Well, it can fall, but it won't bend—return to Paris, denounce me at the bench—that's your job. Mine is to take Toulon, and I will take it. I swear by my name.

FRÉRON

And what is your name?

BONAPARTE

Napoléon Bonaparte.

(The drum beats in the camp. One hears the cry of "Long Live the Republic.")

ALBITTI

What is that?

BONAPARTE

Nothing. The new general has arrived.

FRÉRON

Who is he?

BONAPARTE

Dugommier.

ALBITTI

And who told you this when we were unaware of it? Dugommier! It's impossible.

BONAPARTE

Listen.

FRÉRON

He's coming this way. Let's go to him. Perhaps he's looking for us.

(enter Dugommier and Gasparin.)

BONAPARTE

No—he's looking for me.

DUGOMMIER

The commander of the artillery?

BONAPARTE

Here I am, Citizen General.

DUGOMMIER

You are a brave young man. Go away citizens, we have to talk.

(returning to Bonaparte)

Gasparin has told me your plan of attack. I approve it entirely. You feel in yourself the power to execute it? If you lack it, I will take it on myself. If it succeeds, I will give you all the honor.

BONAPARTE

I will answer for it.

DUGOMMIER

Then give your orders.

BONAPARTE

We are going to attack?

DUGOMMIER

Right away.

BONAPARTE

Cannoneers, send up a signal rocket.

(rocket goes up)

DUGOMMIER

What are you going to do?

BONAPARTE

Wait!

(A moment of silence, then a huge explosion in Toulon)

Now the city is too busy with its own affairs to meddle with ours.

DUGOMMIER

Citizen soldiers, obey the orders of this commander as if they were mine.

BONAPARTE

The army will divide in four columns. Two will watch Forts Malbousquit, Balagnier, and l'Equilette. Another will stay in reserve to support the others whenever danger arises. The fourth will have the honor to march under the orders of the general in chief. Captain Muison, who knows these localities, will lead the avant-garde with a battalion; meanwhile, I will throw several hundred bombs on little Gibraltar.

(drums)

Ah—there's our English cousins waking up. Come on, children, long live liberty, long live the Republic!

ALL THE SOLDIERS

Long live the Republic!

BONAPARTE

Commence firing.

THE CANNONEERS

Load—fire.

DUGOMMIER

Citizen Representatives, come and thank this young man for if one is ungrateful to him, I warn you, he's going to go far beyond us all. Come, children, to the charge.

ALL THE SOLDIERS

Long live the Republic.

DUGOMMIER

Forward—the Marseillaise.

(They go out singing the Marseillaise.)

CURTAIN

ACT II

Tableau 2

The Forest of St. Cloud—barracks, puppet shows, cafes, etc.

(A mountebank on a stool, pointing alternately to two pictures with a long pointer)

MOUNTEBANK

Come in, come in, citizens. You will see the famous battle of the pyramids won by General-in-Chief Bonaparte over the ferocious Mourad-Bey, the most powerful leader of the Mameluks. Also, you can see the battle of Marengo, won by the First-Consul Bonaparte. You will notice in the corner at the left, the death of Citizen General Desaix who fell in the arms of his aide de camp saying these memorable words: "Go tell the First Consul that I die with regret that I have not done enough for the Republic," Come in, come in, Citizens—don't pay till after you have seen and, if you don't like it, we ask nothing from you—absolutely nothing, nothing at all. Come in, come in, citizens.

LABREDÈCHE

It's really the likeness of the great man!

MOUNTEBANK

Perfect.

LABREDÈCHE

I must go in—and with enthusiasm. They tell me the First Consul knows everything said about him, good or bad. This will be a note for my petition.

MOUNTEBANK

(to Lorrain)

Pardon, citizen, one cannot go in here with a lit pipe.

LORRAIN

How's that, you dandy, one cannot go in with a pipe? Do you know that with this pipe I went into an Egyptian palace, and that your little hut and all your furniture wouldn't fill the air hole from its cellar.

MOUNTEBANK

It's possible because in Egypt, everyone smokes.

LABREDÈCHE

That's right.

MOUNTEBANK

But here it annoys people.

LABREDÈCHE

It's exactly as you say. What more do you intend to do?

(He enters)

MERCHANT

Buy, buy, citizens! Handsome umbrella. Citizen, a handsome cape.

CRIER

Look what's just appeared. It's the route of march for the ceremonies that will take place tomorrow for the crowning of First Consul Bonaparte, under the name of Napoléon I, First Emperor of the French, with details of the streets through which the cortege will pass. This has just appeared in the *Monitor*—it's the details....

PASSERBY

How much?

CRIER

Two sous! Here's what has just appeared.

PASSERBY

(aside)

That's good to know. If I don't succeed. This evening, well to-morrow, by a window in a garret, we will see. He ought to be here at 7:30.

(giving his papers to a man of the people)

Well, what do you say to that, eh?

MAN

I said it will be a fine ceremony.

PASSERBY

Are you happy over it?

MAN

Yes, I believe so—there's a free distribution.

PASSERBY

And it is on the people that we count. From what Faubourg are you, citizen?

MAN

Faubourg Saint Marceau—known in the revolution.

PASSERBY

And what does your very republican Faubourg think?

MAN

It is content.

PASSERBY

And it sees its liberty taken away tranquilly.

MAN

You see, citizen, liberty is bread at two sous per pound. There's work and one pays in cash. Long Live Liberty and the Emperor Napoléon! That's all I know.

PASSERBY

Wretches! Wretches! Not a word for their legitimate sovereign.

MERCHANT

Buy, buy, buy!

PASSERBY

(following with his eyes a man in the crowd)

Is it he? Saint Regent and Carbon?

SECOND PASSERBY

Cerachies and Arena.

FIRST PASSERBY

Is it you?—well—what news?

SECOND PASSERBY

I've taken a ticket for George Cadoudal.

FIRST PASSERBY

What?

SECOND PASSERBY

For his trouble. I told him that tonight, we have a rendezvous here, that Bonaparte is coming sometime, disguised, to learn the opinion of the people, and that we can join him. Then—he knows us.

FIRST PASSERBY

And Moreau?

SECOND PASSERBY

Ah, Moreau. There's no use waiting for him. He's too delicate, too grand of soul. We came to relieve the soldiers in his favor— all ways of escape were prepared and he refused to profit by it— he intends to be judge. As for our Polish Brethren….

FIRST PASSERBY

Bah! There's not an instant to lose. Tomorrow they crown him, he is going to pardon the conspirators, this will ruin the Royalist party and depopularize it more. And then the silk stockings have no way to conspire. Listen. One of us will follow him if he comes here this evening, and at the moment when he strikes him the other will cry thief, and the other—along the route.

(Perceiving the spy who prowls around him)

That man is always looking at us. Come.

CRIER

Behold what's just appeared, etc.

LABREDÈCHE

(getting out of the barracks)

Wait—my friend, enchanted, it is impossible not to recognize him, when one has the happiness to see the great man but once in person. I believe that there is a man who will listen to me.

LORRAIN

(leaving)

I tell you, I won't pay.

MOUNTEBANK

Why?

LORRAIN

Because you said one needn't pay if one was not satisfied and I am not satisfied at all. It isn't worth two sous—and the proof....

(returning)

Boy, a small glass.

(he drinks the little glass and pays)

You see, indeed it's not for the two sous. But you have made pyramids which choke me, stupid fool and then of Marengo the First Consul is not well portrayed.

(Bonaparte and Duroc enter.)

LORRAIN

Oh! You don't have to convince me at least! And tell me that he had black eyes when they were, in fact, blue. I saw him in Toulon when he said, "These batteries will not move from this place." I saw him at the pyramids when he said "From the tops of these monuments, forty centuries observe you." And you understand that after having been contemplated by forty centuries, you are likely to frighten me—understand pasty face, I saw him on the 18 Brumaire when they came to murder him—and when Marat told us—"Grenadiers, there are at least five hundred lawyers who say Bonaparte is a…."—they lied! What I say. Well then said he—"Forward, march, Grenadiers, and force the lawyers to evacuate." It was not long. And he's going to tell me, what Bonaparte looks like when I saw him at least twenty times just like I see you face to face.

(seeing Bonaparte)

Stupid, stupid—fool.

BONAPARTE

Hush and pay.

(to a merchant)

Well—how's business?

MERCHANT

Fine. It's getting back. Oh! It was time for the First Consul to decide to make himself Emperor.

BONAPARTE

The whole world is satisfied then?

MERCHANT

I really believe so.

BONAPARTE

(to Duroc)

You see Duroc…?

(to merchant)

…and the Bourbons?

MERCHANT

Bah! Who thinks of them?

BONAPARTE

There are always conspiracies.

MERCHANT

Yes, because, until he was Emperor and the succession was not settled in his family, they hoped to return if they assassinated him. But when one must assassinate his three brothers—the whole world—bah! And yet, the First Consul is wrong. He exposes himself too much. They say at night he goes out disguised. Well—what prevents an assassin?

DUROC

The Citizen is right; the First Consul is wrong. You understand?

BONAPARTE

Yes—but isn't this the way to learn what people really think of me? Don't you realize that the imaginary danger that I run is well purchased by the pleasure of listening to my praise, to see all the nation regard me as a savior? Duroc, when one day perhaps they call me a usurper, I will have the need for the voice of my conscience to say "The sole legitimate sovereign is the nation's choice and who more than you is the legitimate sovereign?"

> (During this time, a man has approached him, drawn a dagger and is about to strike when the spy throws himself between them.)

DUROC

Assassin!

SPY

(who has deflected the blow)

One throws one self before the knife, one receives the blow, and one doesn't cry out.

BONAPARTE

Silence! I am going to be recognized in the midst of this tumult. Give your purse to this man who has saved me, and ask his name. Till tomorrow, at the Tuileries.

DUROC

(to the Spy)

The person you have saved desires to know your name?

SPY

Have I asked his?

DUROC

Here's his purse.

SPY

(showing his arm!)

Here's my blood!

DUROC

Take it.

SPY

(throwing the purse to the people)

Here my friends, drink to the health of the First Consul. It was he who was just now among you.

ALL

Long live the First Consul!

BLACKOUT

ACT II

Tableau 3

An apartment in the Tuileries.

CHARLES

(entering)

Nine-thirty: the First Consul is late.

JOSÉPHINE

(at the door) Charles! Charles

CHARLES

Ah, madame!

JOSÉPHINE

My husband has not yet left his chamber?

CHARLES

You know he told me not to wake him unless I had bad news and today I've only good news.

JOSÉPHINE

For everybody?

CHARLES

Yes.

JOSÉPHINE

(eagerly)

He signed it?

CHARLES

Yesterday.

JOSÉPHINE

And did he grumble?

CHARLES

A little—he felt that six hundred thousand francs debt in six months....

JOSÉPHINE

Nine months.

CHARLES

Well—nine months—he found, I say....

JOSÉPHINE

Charles, if he knew.

CHARLES

Ah, madam, what are you going to tell me?

JOSÉPHINE

Charles, you who are his friend since college—

CHARLES

Oh my god, you terrify me.

JOSÉPHINE

If he knew that I hadn't dared to admit...

CHARLES

The three quarters—the two....

JOSÉPHINE

(low voice)

The half....

CHARLES

Twelve hundred thousand francs of debts. Do you know what the nation grants the First Consul?

JOSÉPHINE

Yes, five hundred thousand francs.

CHARLES

Well, this includes all pensions, bonuses, special funds—all is covered there.

JOSÉPHINE

Charles, I swear to you, it isn't my fault.

CHARLES

Let's see—in good conscience! I've seen a memo from Leroy. Thirty-four hats in one month.

JOSÉPHINE

Ah, you know that Bonaparte doesn't like to see me wear the same hat all the time.

CHARLES

Yes, but thirty-four in one month: so you can wear two per day.

JOSÉPHINE

No, but the clothiers torment me—they send me boxes full of objects of the best taste. I don't know which to select; they tell me to take them all as if they didn't need any money. I let myself be tempted, then without my knowing it—it adds up to enormous sums.

CHARLES

Twelve hundred thousand francs!

JOSÉPHINE

Oh, beside—all that wasn't for my clothes. Don't I have my pensions also? My widows, my orphans? A hand turned towards me can it be sent away empty?

CHARLES

Yes, I know that you are kind.

JOSÉPHINE

If you knew how fine it feels to give! Can I tell them to pray for the First Consul—for me.

CHARLES

For you! And could you want to?

JOSÉPHINE

Charles—I am sometimes very unhappy—ah, it's not Bonaparte who—no, you know that he is good to me! But, Emperor, Emperor—will he always be the master? Charles, has he ever spoken to you of divorce?

CHARLES

Never.

JOSÉPHINE

Oh, if he spoke to you of it, Charles, in the name of heaven, in the name of that which is most sacred in the world—oh. Ah, there he is. I'm going to escape. Charles, don't speak to him of the 600,000 francs that remain. Later! Much later!

CHARLES

And the weight on the Treasury?

JOSÉPHINE

Oh—let me forget.

(Exit Joséphine After a moment Bonaparte enters with an usher)

BONAPARTE

(to the usher)

A man will come this morning. He will say two words: "Toulon and Liberty". You will bring him to me by this door.

(the usher leaves)

Sit down Charles—we will have work to do today. Have you the papers? What do they say?

CHARLES

The French papers?

BONAPARTE

No they say only what I wish. I know in advance what's in them. The foreign papers?

CHARLES

The English papers speak of war and protest their love of peace.

BONAPARTE

Their love for peace! And why then, don't they observe the treaty of Amiens? Why do they refuse, against all their promises to protect Malta, the storehouse of the Mediterranean, the resupply point for Egypt? I would much prefer to abandon the Faubourg Saint Antoine to them!

(Enter the usher with the Spy)

USHER

Here's someone who waits to see the First Consul.

(the spy enters enveloped in a cape. Charles wishes to withdraw, Bonaparte signals him to stay)

BONAPARTE

Well, what news?

SPY

(pointing the Charles)

We are not alone.

BONAPARTE

Speak low. What do they say of the coronation?

SPY

That is the general wish.

BONAPARTE

And the Jacobins? Are they still plotting?

SPY

You are forewarned against them: neither the Jacobins nor the republicans are to be feared: it's the royalists.

BONAPARTE

No matter—my police are not good.

SPY

I believe it.

BONAPARTE

I just missed being assassinated yesterday at St. Cloud.

SPY

I know it.

BONAPARTE

How?

SPY

I was there.

BONAPARTE

Who sent you?

SPY

No one.

BONAPARTE

A man saved my life.

SPY

By throwing himself before the assassin.

BONAPARTE

He received a blow.

(The spy opens his cloak and shows his arm.)

BONAPARTE

In the arm.

(After a silence.)

BONAPARTE

What, it was you?

SPY

You see that a spy can be of use just as the police—when there is nothing to be gained from a dagger.

BONAPARTE

What can I do for you? What do you want?

SPY

For me? And what are the titles or ranks bestowed on a spy? One gives them money—and you don't let me lack that or one gives them orders—I wait on yours.

BONAPARTE

Well then, go back to the neediest of the populace, to whom I am going in an hour. Go through the crowd to Notre-Dame. Say that the Emperor Napoléon will love his subjects better than the First Consul loved his citizens. Say—say whatever your devotion to me inspires you to.

(The spy leaves)

What a strange fellow he is!

BONAPARTE

It's useless for you to say, my dear secretary, that France has had enough of the Republic. The Directory has done more against it than the Mountain. And you see that it remains full of old Romans. Of 3,374,688 votes, 2,569 only are negative. You see there that it is France itself which gives me the title Emperor, not I who take it.

CHARLES

You Majesty, no matter what you do—

BONAPARTE

No, no, keep saying Citizen First Consul:

(looking at his watch)

You have one more hour to be a republican—well—what were you saying?

CHARLES

I said, Citizen First Consul, that no matter what you do, the Kings of Europe will always regard you as their inferior.

BONAPARTE

Well, I will dethrone them all—and then I will be the Elder.

CHARLES

Take care, if you remake the bed of the Bourbons, not to sleep in ten years.

BONAPARTE

My dear secretary! Give me the list of Marshals of the Empire—
so I may sign it. Read the names.

CHARLES

Berthier, Murat, Morcey, Jaurdan, Masséna, Augereau, Bernad-
otte, Soult, Brune, Launes, Mortier, Ney, Davout, Bessières, Kel-
lerman, Lefebre, Pérignon, and Sérurier.

BONAPARTE

Eighteen republicans! Well, you will see if one refuses the baton
of Marshal, because it is given to him from the hand of an Emperor. I have only one regret today. It is to be unable to join to
this list of names, the names of Desaix and Kléber. Your miserable Directory! If they had not forgotten me or rather kept me
confined in Egypt. If they had sent me, as they had sworn to do,
men and money I wouldn't have returned like a fugitive. It is true
that happened. I have taken my revenge. What immense projects
that hovel of Saint Jean d'Acre has reversed! If I had taken it, if
I had found in the city the treasure of the Pasha and weapons for
300,000 men! I would have raised and armed Syria. I'd have
marched on Damascus and Aleppo; I'd have enlarged my army
with all the Christians and Druses and with the malcontents I'd
recruited. I would have moved inland with massive armies. I'd
have arrived at Constantinople. In place of the Turkish Empire I
would have founded a new and greater Empire which would
have fixed my place in history, and perhaps I would have returned to Paris by way of Adrianople or Vienna after having an-
nihilated the house of Austria. All that could have been and now
all that must be done over.

(a silence)

How many invasion ships has the Port of Boulogne?

CHARLES

Nine hundred! And when is our entry into London?

BONAPARTE

I don't know yet. Oh! It's by way of India that one attacks England—it's in her commerce and not in her government—that she must be weakened. When I am master of all the ports on the Mediterranean and the Ocean, when under pain of disobeying my will they cannot receive an English sail—we shall see.

CHARLES

But for that, you must have a European monarch.

BONAPARTE

(starting to scribble)

Yes, when I have that! Fool that I am! These are the best pens.

CHARLES

Those I have sharpened myself. Since I must decipher your writing, it is in my interest that you write as legibly as possible.

BONAPARTE

Yes, Yes.

(watching him fixedly)

What do you think of me Charles?

CHARLES

Why I think you resemble a facile architect. You build behind a scaffold that you will let fall when you are finished.

BONAPARTE

You are right. I didn't see that in two years. Write. "The Polytechnic School will henceforth receive an entirely military organization. The students will wear uniforms and the barracks be subject to discipline." I intend to make a nursery for great men. These will be generals for my successor. I've done well to remove a letter from my name: I gain a signature on nine.

CHARLES

You wish to sign?

(The sound of clocks is heard)

BONAPARTE

Let me hear the sound of the clocks. You know how much I love it.

CHARLES

Especially to the sound of those which tell you that in half an hour, the First Consul Bonaparte will be the Emperor Napoléon.

BONAPARTE

You are mistaken. They remind me of my first years at Brienne. I was happy then.

(Enter Joséphine)

BONAPARTE

Well, what are you doing here, Joséphine? Will you leave us, Charles?

(Charles Leaves)

BONAPARTE

You are not yet in costume.

JOSÉPHINE

No, no my friend. This imperial mantle costs me something to wear. Oh tell me, don't you have ominous feelings?

BONAPARTE

Me? No—and what kind?

JOSÉPHINE

Don't you fear that fortune will not favor you under this new title? Fortune will find you under a tent, but you look for it on a throne.

BONAPARTE

Child! Eh! Will I ever be anything but the soldier of Toulon, the General of Areble, or the Consul of Marengo? My fortune will always follow me—why do you wish to stop me when I am going to touch the end? Why won't Bonaparte's star shine for Napoléon?

JOSÉPHINE

Oh—aren't you grand enough?

BONAPARTE

Do you believe it was a vain ambition which made me desire a new title? Be advised, I don't over estimate my own worth. Or do you think that the imperial mantle or the hand of justice will give me a higher opinion of myself? Europe is old and my mission is to regenerate it. I must accomplish this. If I didn't wish to be emperor, even so, the people would elevate me in spite of myself to the imperial shield. I do wish it, because, at the same time, I alone can save France, and I alone can consolidate it. As a general, a bullet could prevent me, and with me would be lost my victories. If I were a Consul, a coup d'état or an assassin's blow could dispose of me as I have disposed of the Directory; Consul for life and an assassin would suffice. And that would-be assassin Cadoudal still waits in the lock-up to be punished for a crime he doesn't even attempt to deny. During the four years of the Consulate, France's life is placed on my head. The Empire and heredity can alone—but I am crazy to discuss politics with you, pretty, pretty, councilor dressed in gauze and lace! No, my Joséphine, no more discussion. It tires your eyes and your mouth and both ought to smile. Assuage the unfortunate, buy silk and incur debts. That's your vocation and don't try to stop mine. It isn't the happiest.

JOSÉPHINE

Pardon! But I still wish to say—

BONAPARTE

What?

JOSÉPHINE

You speak of heredity? For whom?

BONAPARTE

I will have a son. Destiny has not led me so high to abandon me suddenly. Perhaps I will be unhappy one day; but it will be when there is nothing left to grant me—having everything, all I will be able to do is descend. My existence is one of those great combinations of fate that fortune intends to complete in its happiness as in its dreams—Joséphine, I will have a son!

JOSÉPHINE

My God! What then is your intention? Listen. I will adopt whoever you wish, any child you present to me saying, "Love him", I will love as I love Eugène—my Eugène! This will be my son—as dear as if I had carried him in my womb.

BONAPARTE

Well—Joséphine, yes, if fate refuses me a son. Yes, I will adopt someone worthy of me, who will have the heart of his mother and the courage of his father. Do you understand me?

JOSÉPHINE

Oh! I dare not hope.

BONAPARTE

Hope.

JOSÉPHINE

Eugène.

BONAPARTE

Eugène Beauharnais.

JOSÉPHINE

Oh my friend! My Bonaparte!

BONAPARTE

Go, my empress! Notre Dame awaits you, and I have a crown to put on your beautiful head.

JOSÉPHINE

(with melancholy)

Friend, I like the flowers of Malmaison better.

(Joséphine leaves.)

BONAPARTE

Excellent, Joséphine! What's the matter, Charles?

CHARLES

(entering)

The Senate comes to beg you to accept the Empire.

BONAPARTE

In an instant, I will receive them.

(Exit Bonaparte)

(Enter Labredèche, Ushers)

LABREDÈCHE

(in the antechamber speaking with an Italian accent)

I tella you I am from the society of our Holy Father, da Pope. A musician of his chapel.

(singing in falsetto)

See! And that I've come to take the orders of his Majesty, the Emperor—I mean to say the First Consul.

CHARLES

(aside)

Oh my God, this man once more! The most intrepid solicitor that I know. And who always has a dead relative, victim of some other government. Well—what is it?

LABREDÈCHE

Ah, Citizen Secretary—let me shake hands with you, citizen ushers—they are veritable jailers. I have been obliged to renounce my French nationality of which I am so proud on this immortal day—in order to get here.

CHARLES

Well sir, here you are—what do you want?

LABREDÈCHE

Don't you recognize me?

CHARLES

On the contrary, I recall you from '98.

LABREDÈCHE

I solicited.

CHARLES

And from 1802.

LABREDÈCHE

I solicited again.

CHARLES

And now again.

LABREDÈCHE

I always solicit. What do you want? It isn't my fault. It, the fault of those who won't give me what I ask. But I hope under the paternal government of his Majesty the Emperor—I will yet obtain justice—for you know that my father.

CHARLES

Yes, yes.

LABREDÈCHE

My unfortunate father is dead—a victim of his devotion to the Republic, combating the Chouans.

CHARLES

Ah! Your father was a Republican?

LABREDÈCHE

No, no.

   (aside)

What the devil have I said—the day of the coronation.

CHARLES

Royalist then?

LABREDÈCHE

Royalist? Still less, sir.

CHARLES

But then he was one or the other?

LABREDÈCHE

He was monarchist, sir.

(aside)

That's the right word.

(aloud)

But not a partisan of the old monarchy, no, no—he dreamed of a new dynasty—a military throne—he said as did Voltaire—"the first became king"—How happy he would be today—if he weren't dead—a victim of—

CHARLES

But you're never been able to support your claims by a death certificate.

LABREDÈCHE

What do you want? The archives burned. I hope to have part of the benefits that will be granted on the occasion of a great day.

CHARLES

But if you are so devoted to the Emperor, why not enlist? His Majesty will have need of men.

LABREDÈCHE

Enlist—me? Me? I am the only child of a widow.

(aside)

Having killed my father, I'd better revive my mother.

(aloud)

But with your protection, Citizen Secretary—if you would—

CHARLES

Give it here.

LABREDÈCHE

Twelve hundred francs—a pension of twelve hundred francs or a place in the bureaucracy

(near the bureau)

When I think that the great man sat here even yesterday—

(returning)

You see a place in the bureaucracy would perhaps be more agreeable than a pension—because in the bureaucracy. A situation of fifteen hundred francs with a little economy, one can put, by six or seven thousand francs on the side.

(dreaming of the bureau)

That it was on this desk he signed his immortal decrees—that this pen, still wet with ink is that with which he will sign my pension. Because, all things considered, I prefer a pension to a place—it doesn't entail hours in an office—it presents itself every trimester—every trimester—right?

CHARLES

Yes.

LABREDÈCHE

Be easy, I will be precise. Sir, you are good enough to tell me that you regard this favor as already granted.

CHARLES

Me? Not at all!

LABREDÈCHE

I beg your pardon indeed—this all escapes you. But you wish avoid my gratitude—you're a fine fellow. If I could show you my soul, you would see it isn't unworthy, sir. Here's the pen— here's the petition—a signature by Bonaparte, I mean to say, by Napoléon—

CHARLES

I will put it before his eyes. That's all I can tell you.

LABREDÈCHE

(aside)

And I will run all the way to Notre Dame to put it before him again because this one will forget me.

(aloud)

Goodbye sir, Goodbye my benefactor! I'm going to join my voice to all those who praise and bless him!

(to usher)

You see I am with the Citizen Secretary: he desires that henceforth I never wait in the antechamber

(Exit Labredèche)

CHARLES

Usher—did you see that gentleman who just left?

USHER

Yes, sir.

CHARLES

Well, remember never to let him enter again.

BLACKOUT

ACT II

Tableau 4

The Garden of the Tuileries.

(Lorrain is seen amongst the people, Bourgeois, soldiers.)

SEVERAL VOICES

There he is! There he is! No—yes—not yet.

VOICES

I tell you that the cortege is going to pass at eleven o'clock precisely. Here's the schedule.

GENTLEMAN

It's eleven-fifteen.

LORRAIN

Say then, have you been charged with making the roll call citizen? It seems to me that he is free to leave when he wishes.

WOMAN

They say that Empress is sick.

LORRAIN

I believe rather it's the Pope. When we had surrounded him at Avignon—he was already very sick, that he made me feel bad.

GENTLEMAN

Oh no—he's very well.

LORRAIN

Ah—he's all right? That's why my commanding officer who commanded his escort was so frightened the Pope would die on his hands. So he got a receipt from the officer of the other escort bringing the Pope to Paris from Avignon. He put on the aforesaid receipt "(Received a pope in bad condition)" That's what good shape he's in. So it's probably His Holiness who makes us all wait.

(Enter Labredèche)

(Then Bonaparte at the Balcony of the Tuileries)

LABREDÈCHE

(to Lorrain)

Not at all, my friend, not at all—it is the Emperor receiving the Senate—Me, I just left the Emperor's office—but for that nothing could have kept me.

PEOPLE

Ah, the window's opening.

GENTLEMEN

He's going to appear—the Emperor is coming to the balcony—here he is—here he is.

LABREDÈCHE

Let me pass.

LORRAIN

Say then citizen you have a sharp elbow I tell you that.

WOMAN

He's dishonest, this man. You see indeed that you cannot pass.

LABREDECHE

The Emperor must see me The Emperor must listen to me.

ALL

Here he is! Here he is!

ALL

Long Live the First Consul!

(Bonaparte salutes the crowd.)

ALL

Long Live the Emperor!

LABREDÈCHE

Long live Napoléon the Great!

LORRAIN

(taking off his hat)

Long live General Bonaparte!

CURTAIN

ACT III

Tableau 5

The interior of the Palace of the King at Dresden.

BONAPARTE

(dictating to Berthier)

Arrived at the Niemen, the army disposes itself thus: at the extreme right leaving from Galicia by way of Droguizzin—Prince Schwarzenberg and 34,000 Austrians—to their left coming from Varsovy and marching through Bialystock and Grodno, the King of Westphalia with 69,200 Westphalian Saxons and Poles, beside them Prince Eugène reuniting, towards Mariendal and Peinoy 79,500 Bavarians, Italians and French, then the Emperor with 220 thousand men commanded by the King of Naples and the Prince d'Eckmuhl, the Dukes of Dantzig, d'Istria, de Reggio, d'Elchingen. Then before Tilsit, MacDonald and 32,500 Prussians, Bavarians, Poles, form the extreme left of the Grand Army.

So Berthier, how many men in motion from the Guadalquiver and the Sea of Calobria to the Vistula?

BERTHIER

617,000.

BONAPARTE

How many infantry?

BERTHIER

420,000.

BONAPARTE

How many bridge pontoons?

BERTHIER

Six.

BONAPARTE

Carriages and food wagons?

BERTHIER

11,000.

BONAPARTE

Cannons?

BERTHIER

1,372.

BONAPARTE

Good.

BERTHIER

And does your Majesty count on the 60,000 Austrians, Prussians, and Spanish who marched in the Army?

BONAPARTE

Yes.

BERTHIER

Your Majesty doesn't fear that they have forgotten Wagram, Jena, and Saragossa?

BONAPARTE

They won't forget, so long as I conquer. One must help one's self by one's conquests to conquer yet again—besides the campaign won't be lengthy. It's a political war, I am attacking the English in Russia. Then they will be quiet—the fifth act, the dénouement. Date my orders from here—from Dresden and send my orders to the papers in Paris. You will come with Caulaincourt, Murat, Ney and our other Marshals.

BERTHIER

Will your Majesty receive this morning the Kings of Württemberg, Prussia, and Westphalia and several others who wish to pay their court to your Majesty?

BONAPARTE

Later! I'm waiting for Talma. Invite them to this spectacle for this evening and I will receive them there. Go!

(Exit Berthier)

(Enter an usher)

USHER

Mr. Talma.

BONAPARTE

Have him come in.

(Talma Enters, the usher leaves)

BONAPARTE

You've been waiting for some time, Talma.

TALMA

Sire, it's not my fault. On entering the court, I found myself in the midst of an embarrassment of Kings from whom I had great trouble in extricating myself.

BONAPARTE

When did you get here?

TALMA

Yesterday evening, sire.

BONAPARTE

Are you too fatigued to play today?

TALMA

No, sire.

BONAPARTE

Remember, you will have a theatre of crowned heads—what news of the Théâtre Français?

TALMA

Some quarrels.

BONAPARTE

Endlessly! Between—?

TALMA

Between the sociétaires for the roles, for the jobs.

BONAPARTE

I will regulate all this from Moscow. Your Republic of the Rue Richelieu gives me more trouble than some kingdoms.

TALMA

And what shall I play? Mahomet?

BONAPARTE

No, no—they will take that as an excuse for an application to me. Besides since I've seen Egypt, I find Voltaire more false than I used to.

TALMA

I have sometimes heard Your Majesty praise Voltaire's Oedipus.

BONAPARTE

The ancient fatality followed him. You see, the entire theatre of Voltaire is a system of which '93 is the last play. But tell me Talma, how do you explain with his hatred for Kings his exaggerated praise for Louis XIV, King of Opera, who fully understood the "mise en scene" of royalty, nothing more, who gave 6,000 francs pension to Boileau and let Corneille die of hunger— Corneille I would have made minister if he had lived in my time.

TALMA

I see I shall play Corneille tonight.

BONAPARTE

Yes, he's always beautiful without ever being false. He aggrandizes the heroes he creates—he doesn't force them to lower themselves to enter the little stairways of Versailles and the doors of L'Oeil de-boeuf. His Greeks are Greeks, his Romans, Romans. They are nude naked arms and legs and don't dress in the livery of Louis XIV.

TALMA

Your Majesty seems to me quite severe.

BONAPARTE

Ah, I don't like your modern literature, Talma. It has taken more trouble to separate itself from its two great models Corneille and Moliere than the Greeks took to resemble Aeschylus and Aristophanes, Legouvé and Belloy had both the intention of giving us a national literature, but like the guardians charged with protecting medieval monuments, who whiten the old statues—sleeping on the old tombs—Du Belloy whitewashes Bayard, and Legouvé regrets Henry IV. When we imitate the Greeks, it must be on Greek subjects and then not discard their beautiful simplicity. Take the Agamemnon of Lemercier. It's not necessary now to come there, Talma, when one speaks of nature. I suppose one day they'll put me in a play. Me! Believe me, I will appear like myself only to the extent I will speak in sonorous phrases and bold gestures, whereas I, poor fellow, have eloquence only by fits and starts, and govern this world with bayonets.

TALMA

Your Majesty must see that your opinion is mine.

BONAPARTE

Yes, yes, you are always simple and natural. Moreover, it's taken a long time for you to be understood. You will play the role of Augustus, Talma—and I wish Czar Alexander were here to hear you say, "Let's be friends, Cinna." Goodbye—here's Caulaincourt, whom I've been asking for.

TALMA

Goodbye sire.

(Enter Caulaincourt)

BONAPARTE

By the way, they said it's you who taught me to hold my throne. It's because of that I play the role so well. Till this evening....

(exit Talma. Napoléon turns to Caulaincourt)

I am not pleased with you, Caulaincourt.

CAULAINCOURT

(advancing)

And how have I had the misfortune to displease Your Majesty?

BONAPARTE

You loudly censure the Russian campaign.

CAULAINCOURT

Yes, sire.

BONAPARTE

And what are your motives? Speak—you know I love to be frank.

CAULAINCOURT

Sire, up to now we have fought only with men and we have won. But Russia! It isn't possible except from June to October. Except for this interval between these two epochs our army is engaged in deserts of mud or ice and perishes entirely without glory. Lithuania is more like Asia than Spain is like Africa. The French won't recognize themselves in a country whose frontier has no limit. They cannot remain without weakening themselves. It is to lose France in Europe, for when Europe becomes France, there will be no more France. Already before the departure of your Majesty, it is left solitary, deserted, without a chief, without an army. Who will defend it then?

BONAPARTE

My renown. I leave it my name and the fear which an armed nation inspires.

CAULAINCOURT

I am not speaking of success—but in case of retreat. Who will support Your Majesty? The Prussians, whom we devoured less than five years ago, and whose alliance is only a feint or forced?

BONAPARTE

Am I not assured of Prussia's tranquility by the care I have taken (leaving no stone unturned) even in the case of a defeat? Do you forget I hold in my hand its police and military? Besides, can I not count on seven Kings who owe me their new titles? Don't six marriages league France with the house of Baden, Bavaria, and Austria? All the sovereigns of Europe ought they not to be as frightened as I am of the military and conquering government of Russia, it's savage population which increases by a half million a year? What means my absence? Different parties in the interior of the Empire? I see only one—that of some royalists. Well, do I really need them? When I subdued them I really wronged myself in the minds of the people? The King of the third estate—not being on the throne it followed I must subdue it as I have done—by glory. A simple citizen as I was, become sovereign as I am— cannot be stopped—he must rise without cease—or he'll fall back down, rest assured, when he remains stationary. These men that my fortune has raised after it had already more than enough for a marshal's baton. It's they who would exchange it for a scepter or a crown. My family tugs at all sides of my imperial mantle—each calls for a throne or at least a grand duchy. It seems to hear my brothers talk that I have devoured the inheritance of the deceased king, our father. Well, the way to contain all these ambitions, to realize all these hopes—is war, always war! And do you believe that I am not bored of war? The Emperor Alexander stands alone facing the summit of the immense edifice I have raised. He stands young, full of life. His forces are augmenting when already mine decrease. He waits only for my death to tear from my cadaver the scepter of Europe. It's necessary that I prevent this danger while Italy, Switzerland, Germany, Prussia and Austria march under my eagles, and that I consolidate the great Empire while disposing of Alexander and the power of Russia, weakened by the loss of all Poland and Borysthenia.

CAULAINCOURT

Your Majesty speaks of his death, and if, on the battlefield, where you are exposed like the least of your soldiers—?

BONAPARTE

You fear the war will end my days? Now is the time of conspiracies. They wanted to frighten me with Cadoudal. He intends to fire on me? Well, he killed my aide-de-camp. When my hour is come, a fever, a fall from a horse in the hunt will kill me as effectively as a bullet. The days are written.

CAULAINCOURT

Sire.

BONAPARTE

(conducting him to a window)

Do you see the height of that star?

CAULAINCOURT

No, sire.

BONAPARTE

Look closely.

CAULAINCOURT

I don't see it, sire.

BONAPARTE

Well, I—I see it. Let's go to the salon. The time for the reception has come.

(The enter the salon at center, the door remains open)

USHER

(announcing)

His Majesty, the King of Saxony.
His Majesty, the King of Württemberg.
His Majesty, the Emperor of Austria.

His Majesty, the King of Naples.
His Majesty, the King of Bavaria.
His Majesty, the King of Prussia.

(As each King enters. Napoléon greets him.)

BLACKOUT

ACT III

Tableau 6

The Heights of Borodino.

(Murat, and an officer at the head of a column.)

SOLDIER

Halt.

MURAT

(to his domestic servant)

Julien, take care of my horse and bring me another. Wash the wound he received in his flank with eau de vie and salt. And get me a saber heavier than this one. These Russians must be split right down the middle before they fall.

SOLDIER

It's very happy to meet them, these scoundrels here. We've marched four hundred leagues and we haven't yet had the pleasure of saying two words to them except at Vitepsk and at Smolensk.

MURAT

I believe they are waiting for us here, my brave ones. Bagration, Barclay, and Koutosof are reunited, and we will have need of luck tomorrow, or I'm much mistaken.

(throwing one of his gloves)

Here, the tent of the Emperor. Here's mine. And you all around us—sleep with your arms and with only one eye shut.

> DOMESTIC

> *(entering)*

Here's the saber Your Majesty asked for—your horse awaits you.

> MURAT

Good—gentlemen, come with me to inspect the flanks.

> *(Exit Murat.)*

> *(The soldiers begin bivouacking.)*

> FIRST SOLDIER

Here's one who has good legs—about time.

> SECOND SOLDIER

They say he intends to become King of the Cossacks.

> THIRD SOLDIER

Bah—and his realm of Naples?

> FIRST SOLDIER

They'll give him another one then! Oh that's it! What is there for the saucepan, children?

> *(turning)*

Tell us then, old veterans, can we ask you for a smoke? These gay dogs! They have great boiled beef broth!

Ah! That's it! You see leave it to the troops and there'll be order everywhere.

(the soldiers open successively their knapsacks)

Flour, flour, and more flour. Well, with that we will have a first course of pudding, and a second course of pudding and a third course of pudding. Thousand gods! In Prussia, in Germany, they always have some turkey and chicken.

(Enter Lorrain, passing an egg in front of his nose)

LORRAIN

What's that you say, there old boy?

FIRST SOLDIER

I say that if it was in our pudding it would give it a famous color.

LORRAIN

(putting the egg in the saucepan)

Well, watch out for a splash and make a place by the fire, place of a soldier. Nothing to it because they cannot read. The space of the hand between the knees—there!

FIRST SOLDIER

Ah, so—but where are you come from? You are not of our squad.

LORRAIN

I've come from Andalusia, and I give the Andalusians to you.

(he blows a kiss)

I didn't tell you that. As for the Spanish men, you see, they're comical—capes which march and swords that never rest—that's all.

FIRST SOLDIER

And what do they eat? Do they eat?

LORRAIN

They eat garlic and chocolate or chocolate and garlic. I don't know exactly. This is called noble like Abraham's thigh. It hasn't a sou in its pocket, it's dry like tinderwood, black like a coal and it smokes like a frying pan. That's your Spaniard.

FIRST SOLDIER

They're a pretty people all the same.

LORRAIN

And the Russians—what are they like? For one must get to know one's new friends.

FIRST SOLDIER

But the Cavalry—that are vulgarly called Cossacks—they're horses with ropes, lances with nails, faces with beards. As to what they eat—one cannot say—one cannot find anything in the country—not even a specimen.

LORRAIN

And the country itself—is it agricultural?

FIRST SOLDIER

Agreeable?

LORRAIN

Agreeable or agricultural, as you prefer.

FIRST SOLDIER

Not at all! For example, this fog has to be cut with a knife.

LORRAIN

Fog—there's a great affair! I've been in some countries where the cavaliers are used only to polish their boots—because of the Poles.

FIRST SOLDIER

(to his neighbor)

What did he say?

SECOND SOLDIER

I don't know. He said the Poles.

THIRD SOLDIER

Bah! Your Spaniards! A pretty people. Not gay at all.

LORRAIN

Not gay. They sing all day.

THIRD SOLDIER

What?

LORRAIN

Vespers.

THIRD SOLDIER

Thanks.

LORRAIN

Listen to me. I'm going to give you an idea of the national song. It's the story of an old Christian—brave man—word of honor. Listen—the refrain and chorus (to Drummer). Let's see—Give your 'la' there.

(he pulls out castanets)

And you too—fife it! Forward, march!
Death surprised in a corner
   The Valorous Don Sancho
He is dead; cup in his snout
   Sleeping on his board.

(with castanets)

Tra, tra, etc.

Son of a proud nobleman.
  Born in Castile
Where—with piety
  His mother died—as a virgin
    Tra, tra, etc.

A quarter of an hour before his death
  His redoubtable father
Named him beneficiary
  Of a fortune he did not have
    Tra, tra, etc.

From scarcity when the wind
  Into his kitchen blew in
He treated himself gravely to
  The tune of a mandolin
    Tra, tra, etc.

The blue and red of flowers
  Shined on his sash
Cupid suspended hearts on the
  Hook of his mustache
    Tra, tra, etc.

This one is sung with crepe on your arm, tears in your eyes
  (with a frown)
To pay for his burial
  His decrepit mistresses
With their rings of gold
  Sold their falsies.

(noise of a drum)

SOLDIER

The Emperor!

ALL

(rising)

The Emperor!

LORRAIN

The Emperor! Sacred dog! It's four years since we last saw each other. We are going to find each other much changed.

(Enter Napoléon, Davout, and his suite.)

BONAPARTE

Good evening boys—good evening. I intend to spend this night with you. It seems then they are going to wait for us.

FIRST SOLDIER

Because they don't evacuate at night from custom.

BONAPARTE

No, no—Murat has recognized their fires. It's a decisive battle boys—like at the Pyramids—my braves—for you were there.

FIRST SOLDIER

A few.

BONAPARTE

(to another)

You remember Austerlitz—it was there you got the Cross….

SECOND SOLDIER

…for having….

BONAPARTE

…captured a flag! Well are you content, my friends? Your captain does he take care of you? Is your money paid on time?

FIRST SOLDIER

Oh, the money is current. It's only the rations that are late.

BONAPARTE

Let's see your soup (*tastes it*). It's good.

FIRST SOLDIER

I believe it! I broke an egg in it. A raw egg which came from the Midi. A sign of cold.

BONAPARTE

(aside)

Yes, a sign of cold.

(aloud)

But we will leave a great fire at Moscow my friend—and we will stay there till spring—I'm thirsty—is there water in the canteen?

LORRAIN

No—but I saw a spring coming here. Wait.

(Lorrain goes out)

BONAPARTE

(to Prince d'Eckmuhl)

Davout, do you know that the retreat of these people astonishes me! All is burned on the way. This resembles a deliberate plan. They say that all their positions have been taken stage by stage from the first. Alexander is silent. I have neglected no opportunity to propose peace to him. It's necessary that I take Moscow to make him decide—if not, we will take winter quarters.

(Enter Lorrain, face covered with blood carrying water)

LORRAIN

Here's water.

BONAPARTE

What happened to you?

LORRAIN

Nothing. I didn't see a ravine and I rolled down. Story of a quick arrival.

BONAPARTE

Wipe off the blood, it prevents seeing your scars.

(After having drunk).

Your water is excellent. Your scars become you. Ah—here's one that I never saw before.

LORRAIN

Ah—it's Spanish. A gift from a senor who sent it to me from behind a hedge. My map to the next world. Happily I stopped halfway there.

BONAPARTE

You cannot read—right?

LORRAIN

No, sire, but it's no shame—it's my father's fault.

BONAPARTE

For brave men like you who don't know how to write, I've created stations as guards of the Eagles. They have the grade of officer. They are those who watch each side of the flag and they have other functions besides defending it. I make you guard of the Eagle of the Sixth.

LORRAIN

Thanks, my Emperor. Come, Come! Here's my marshal's baton.

(Napoléon retires under his tent with Davout. Then Murat enters.)

BONAPARTE

Ah, there you are, Murat. Well?

MURAT

They are holding. The forts stretch the length of the Moscova River. All this indicates that tomorrow we will find them in their trenches.

BONAPARTE

It will be an artillery battle that decides things—so much the better.

MURAT

(to Davout)

Speaking of artillery, prince—yesterday one of your batteries refused to fire on my express order. Why?

DAVOUT

Because I manage my soldiers and I don't shed their blood except when it's absolutely necessary.

MURAT

Yes, you are prudent.

DAVOUT

And Your Majesty is too daring—besides we'll see what remains of your cavalry at the end of the campaign. It belongs to you and you can dispose of it—as for the Infantry of the 1st Corps, it will be under my orders, and I will not allow it to be squandered.

MURAT

Do you forget that if you command the Infantry I command you?
The Emperor has placed you under my orders.

DAVOUT

Your Majesty condescends to battle with a simple Marshal?

MURAT

I even battle with a Cossack.

BONAPARTE

(rolling a bullet with his foot)

That's enough gentlemen—I desire that in the future you work
better together, for you are both necessary to me. Murat with his
boldness and you Davout with your prudence. Go get your
sleep—you won't find it useless for tomorrow's work.

(they leave)

This will be a terrible battle—but I have 80,000 men. I will lose
20,000. I will enter Moscow with 60,000; the trainees will rejoin
us, then the marching battalions and we will be stronger than before the battle. Four hours from dawn. All sleep. Only I watch
with my thoughts—thoughts of war and destruction! Oh sleep,
children, dream of your mothers and your country—tomorrow
thousands of you will be sleeping again but on frozen and bloody
earth.

(pause)

What a strange fortune is mine! A man as obscure as they are—
who leads in his wake millions of men! Oh, there are moments
when I am alone, face to face with my genius, I tremble because
I doubt! If I believed that my star was only audacity and my genius—chance. What a frightful responsibility—a life that so many
million men will rise one day, bloody and mutilated to accuse me
before God and say, "You had no mission to do what you have
done—so let the tears and the blood fall back on your head."
Oh—it's impossible! What men! Don't they speak of a race apart
having several existences to lose? It's thirteen years since with

them I tested the Orient through Egypt and broke them against it's gates. In the interval we've conquered Europe—and here they are coming from the North into Asia to be broken again, perhaps? Who has shoved them into this wandering and adventurous life? They are not barbarians seeking for better climates, better living conditions, spectacles more drunken—on the contrary, they possess all their wealth, they have abandoned it to live without shelter, without bread, and to fall each successive day— dead or mutilated on the road I travel—which embraces the circle of the globe that I sow with graves and that leads to immortality, to nothingness.

(one hears the reveille)

The day—already day.

(everybody is up)

Well, Duroc?

(Enter Duroc, followed by several Marshals.)

DUROC

The enemy is holding his position.

BONAPARTE

Let's attack! My friend—there's the Sun of Austerlitz.

MURAT

What are Your Majesty's orders?

BONAPARTE

(to the Marshals who surround him)

Here's the general plan! During the combat my aides de camps will carry my special orders to you. Eugène will be the pivot. The right will engage first. Under cover of the woods it will take the opposing forts, it will move to it's left, working on the Russian Flank, rolling and driving back all their army on their right and into the Kalouga. Three batteries of cannons each will be trained on the Russian forts, two on their left and one on the center. Poniatowski and his army will advance by the Old Smolensk road—you will wait for his first cannon fire. That will be the signal. Go, gentlemen!

SOLDIERS

Here's the battle!

BONAPARTE

You've wanted it so much. From now on the Victory depends on you. We need it. It will give you abundance—good winter quarters and a prompt return home. Behave as you did at Austerlitz, at Friedland, at Vitepsk and at Smolensk. Let our most distant posterity cite your conduct this day—so they will say of you—"He was at this great battle before the gates of Moscow."

BLACKOUT

ACT III

Tableau 7

In Moscow—a hall in the Kremlin.

BONAPARTE

(entering with his Marshals)

Moscow empty! Moscow deserted—are you quite sure? Go Murat—and try to discover some inhabitants. Here all is new—we for them, they for us—perhaps they don't know how to surrender. Not the least smoke, not the least noise—it's the immobility of Thebes—the silence of the desert. Trévise at the time of pillage! You will answer to me with your head. Here I am the, in Moscow—in the ancient place of the Czar—in the Kremlin! It was time. Where is Murat?

A MARSHAL

At the head of his cavalry pursuing the Russian rear guard on the way to Vladimir.

BONAPARTE

I love him, this Murat! Always ardent, tireless, as in Italy as in Egypt. Six hundred leagues and sixty battles haven't tired him. He crosses Moscow without stopping at the Kremlin—where I stopped I!—Are you all cold, gentlemen? Do you realize where we are?

BERTHIER

Yes, Sire, 600 leagues from Paris, with an army diminished by 40,000 men by the Battle of Moscow—without supplies, clothes, munitions.

BONAPARTE

Well—aren't we in the enemy's capital? Moscow widow of 300,000 inhabitants, you appear too small to lodge 80,000 men? These palaces that you share between you—are they less sumptuous or less agreeable than the hotels of the Faubourg Saint Honoré—or the Quai d'Orsay? As for me, I admit, that I prefer my Tuileries and my Louvre but for this winter, I will content myself with the palace of the Romanovs and Rurik.

VOICES

(outside)

A Frenchman, a Frenchman.

BONAPARTE

Do you hear? A Frenchman—bring him here—so I can learn something of this bizarre secret. Moscow deserted.

(perceiving the Spy)

Ah, it's you.

SPY

(entering)

Yes, Sire.

BONAPARTE

Where are you coming from?

SPY

Prison.

BONAPARTE

From prison?

SPY

I was recognized as French and arrested at Moscow when Your Majesty had passed the Niemen.

BONAPARTE

Is it true that the City is deserted?

SPY

I saw the last Russians leave by the Kolonina Gate.

BONAPARTE

Ah! The Russians don't yet realize the effect that will be produced on them by the loss of their capital. You have heard him, gentlemen. Moscow is ours, entirely ours. Let each establish his quarters in the part of the city that pleases him but with order. Think that this is our Paris for this winter. Go, gentlemen, and send me the work from Paris. I haven't worked on that since Smolensk. Starting from today my decrees will be dated from the Kremlin.

(they leave—to the Spy)

Well—what have you seen in this Russia?

SPY

A people bitter and hard like its earth—molded for slavery, ignorant for another century at least, and suppressing civilization as others suppress despotism.

BONAPARTE

Yes, yes, and still more dangerous because the will of one man moves these enormous masses. Misfortune, misfortune for Europe if I don't stifle this colossus to the heart, for if I fail who will kill it? But from here I watch, sentinel of civilization, one foot in Asia, one foot in Europe. Children! They haven't seen in my desire to arrive in Moscow anything but vanity to sign a decree dated from the holy city, seated on the throne of Russia and sheltered by the gold cross of the Great Ivan.

God give me the time and the strength and I will make Moscow one of the ports of entry into my European realm. From here I will call the universe to civilization as the muezzin calls the Mahometans to prayer from the height of the minarets. And then (looking around him) what voice will rise to say, "Isn't Napoléon the envoy of God?" And when I think that if I did not reach this Moscow, being stopped by a fever, a fall from a horse, a bullet— and that they believed this proud alliance to be an ordinary war, a quarrel between the Emperor and Emperor, a vulgar invasion of territory—

SPY

Bonaparte, Napoléon, it isn't I, at least, who you will accuse of not having understood you.

BONAPARTE

No, no, I know it, and I do you justice. But go, here's the Paris portfolio, and my minister travels with me.

(Exit Spy, enter the Minister.)

BONAPARTE

Have you prepared the three decrees I asked of you?

MINISTER

Yes, Sire.

BONAPARTE

Let's see what we have here.

MINISTER

It is relative to pawn shops actually existing in the city of Florence.

BONAPARTE

Ah, it's prohibition against receiving any deposit and of loaning on security isn't it? Add: "The municipal pawnshop of the city of Florence is preserved—all acts relative to its establishment will be exempt from tax and registration". In this manner, one can loan eight percent to the unfortunate and not ruin them by charging them fifteen to twenty. What is that?

MINISTER

The creation of a special fund for the execution of work restoring and enlarging the Gardon canal..

BONAPARTE

Well—with God's help. I hope in ten years. France will be traversed in every way by thirty navigable canals. And this here?

MINISTER

A rule on the Théâtre Français on the employment of sociétaires, on their pensions, on that of Talma whose stipend raised to 30,000 francs.

BONAPARTE

Give it here. If we spend the winter in Moscow I intend to have half of my troops here—I will order him to be here by the end of October. What's that? It cannot be day again?

VOICES

(outside)

Fire—fire.

BONAPARTE

(hurling himself towards the window)

Fire in the merchant's palace in the center of the city in its richest quarter—misfortune! It's some drunken soldier who'll burn us in a palace.

MORTIER

(entering)

Sire, Sire—fire!

BONAPARTE

Well, I know it, I can see it from here. Ah! I'm not deceived—from there towards the Dorogonulof Gate—more fire—Trévise, well—you see it, I place you in charge of the city police. I give you Moscow, the rich sleeping Moscow—in your hands—and on all sides flames are surging.

MORTIER

Sire, I know, but the flames are coming from houses boarded up—the fire comes from within—

BONAPARTE

The fire's been set. Yes, by some pillager who wants to separate gold from stuffing—oh—look, look and get help.

MURAT

(entering)

Sire, the pumps are broken. It's a plot. It's the Russians who are burning us—they have turned Moscow into an infernal machine.

BONAPARTE

You see the fire spreads! Is the wind an accomplice?

SPY

(entering)

Sire, Sire, pardon! Everything is burning—all is on fire.

BONAPARTE

Who's burning the city? Who set the fire?

SPY

The Russians! The Muzhiks.

BONAPARTE

Impossible.

SPY

Look, I can see them running in the middle of this furnace.

BONAPARTE

Put the fire out—kill them like wild beasts. But this city is built of wood and resin.

VOICES

(outside)

The fire at the Kremlin. The fire.

MURAT

Let us leave, Sire, let us leave.

BONAPARTE

Oh, stay Gentlemen. You aren't afraid this palace will fall on your head? Stay and listen: To the struggle with the flames of Moscow lit by the Russians, eternal war with the Russians. They drive us from their first capital—follow them to the second. Let it burn and listen to me.

SOLDIERS

(outside)

The Emperor, the Emperor.

BONAPARTE

(at the window)

Here I am boys, fear nothing. I watch over you and God watches over me. Let it burn gentlemen and if the fire spares something—annihilate what the fire spares. Counting from now, Moscow no longer exists on the map of the world. Russia has only one capital—Saint Petersburg, and in twelve days we will be there.

ALL

Saint Petersburg.

A MARSHAL

Sire, what are you thinking of? St. Petersburg? Impossible!

BONAPARTE

Are you soldiers of fortune, children of war, astonished by a great resolution? Don't you see we are totally lost if we retreat? The winter, the bitter winter of Russia will seize us—halfway on the road to France.

ANOTHER MARSHAL

Sire, Sire, the fire!

BONAPARTE

And what will you do then? My soldiers, my boys, what will they do when your hands freeze on the points of your sabers, and the cannon? When they fall at each step and cannot get up again? When they must retreat by a route devastated by their passage? Our strength is more moral than material, prestige surrounds us! Up to the present we are invincible. A step back and the prestige is destroyed.

(pushing his hand on a map)

Here's Moscow, Paris, and St. Petersburg—look and choose.

MARSHALS

Paris.

BONAPARTE

Ah, yes, Paris! There are splendid hotels, coaches with six horses, your royal lands. Paris—and when you get there—this Paris will make you timid, cowardly, traitorous?

A MARSHAL

Sire, the fire, the fire—we cannot stay here!

BONAPARTE

(stamping his foot)

I can stay here quite well myself—and destroy rather than leave to return to France! To St. Petersburg then, there, peace, glory, the regards of the world, the applause of the universe! No, you won't do it? Well kill the most gigantic project which was born in the skull of a man. You don't realize that in separating me from Moscow you are tearing me from the world.

(he tears the map)

You want to retreat? Well you will have it. And on you will fall all the misfortunes of this funereal retreat. Go—arrange it and leave me. Ah, leave me. I tell you—I order you and I mean it.

(The Marshals leave)

BONAPARTE

Oh, it is a sea of fire. Human weakness—the breath of God above could light this fire. Oh Napoléon—you think yourself more than man, because you cover half the world with tents and with soldiers, because at only a word from you kings tremble and thrones overturn. Well you are weak, without power in the face of this conflagration. Each foot of earth that it wins devours your empire, Napoléon! Napoléon! Well try your power, order this fire to be extinguished, for this conflagration to retreat, and if it obeys you, you are more than man—you are simply a God. Oh, my most beautiful provinces for Moscow! Rome, Naples, Florence, my entire Italy, I can take it back; but Moscow, Moscow—never!

SPY

(rushing in)

Sire, in the name of heaven! Sire, the Kremlin is mined! My God, the stairs crack, the gates are glowing. You are under a heaven of fire, an earth of fire between walls of fire.

BONAPARTE

Moscow! Moscow!

SPY

(turning towards the door)

Grenadiers, to me, to the Emperor! Save the Emperor. He doesn't wish to leave and the Kremlin is mined.

(The Grenadiers enter. Napoléon turns toward them calmly.)

BONAPARTE

Soldiers, take down the Golden cross of Ivan the Great—it will go well on the dome of the Invalides.

(he leaves)

BLACKOUT

ACT III

Tableau 8

A hovel on the banks of the Beresina.

(The Spy enters, long beard and covered with icicles and snow.)

SPY

A hovel! At least Napoléon will have some shelter for the night. What times! What a country! Desolation—ah there is a fire. The Cossacks have hardly abandoned it—but how to relight it.

(tearing a window slatter)

Good! This outside slatter! My cloak will replace it.

(he relights the fire—hangs his cloak before the window)

YOUNG MAN

(firing at the door)

Fire! Pity. Help!

SPY

(taking his weapon)

Get out—this is the Emperor's cabin.

YOUNG MAN

Oh! in the name of the Emperor—grace—grace—I am a woman.

SPY

A woman?

WOMAN

Yes, yes. Will you save me if I am a woman?

SPY

Come here—and warm up.

WOMAN

You have nothing to give me?

SPY

Some drops of wine.

(giving her a gourd)

What you leave will be for the Emperor—he is saved, isn't he?

WOMAN

Yes—for a time. You didn't know the bridge gave way?

SPY

Yes, yes, I know it.

(to some military who wish to enter)

Get back—this is the Emperor's cabin.

SOLDIERS

Let's go further.

WOMAN

And do you believe that the Emperor will find this cabin?

SPY

(taking a brand and waving it before the door)

The Emperor, the Emperor.

SOLDIERS

(in the distance)

Ha!

OTHER SOLDIERS

(to the Spy)

Comrade—fire huh? Give us some fire.

SPY

Take some.

(they take the fire and leave)

SOLDIERS

(outside)

Have you some wood—where is there wood?

BONAPARTE

(at the door)

My friends—demolish this cabin—take the thatch roof which covers it—make fires, make fires!

SOLDIERS

And you? And Your Majesty?

BONAPARTE

(removing his glove and taking their hands)

Me—I'm hot—hold on.

FIRST SOLDIER

No Sire, we much prefer to die.

NAPOLÉON

My children.

SPY

Go on!

BONAPARTE

Let the guards of the Eagles enter—they must warm their hands to hold their flags.

(the Flag and Eagle Guards enter)

LORRAIN

(to the Spy)

Oh! If you please, Comrade—a little place by the fire, place for a sub officer—sacred rascal—I have hands swollen like gourds. Tell me Comrade, can one ask you without indiscretion? What you have frozen?

SPY

Nothing.

LORRAIN

You are very happy! Do me the pleasure of saying that I still have my nose—I no longer sense it since Smolensk. And with that I'm hungry. Come, come, we will notch our belts. I've dined.

BONAPARTE

The cannon! The cannon! It's Kutuzov's advance guard and Wittgenstein who has joined my rear guard. But Ney is there—Ney, the bravest of the brave! Charles XII, Charles XII!

(to the Aide de Corps)

Well, the cannons have changed direction. Whose cannon?

AIDE DE CORPS

Thitchikov with 30,000 men is attacking our flank.

BONAPARTE

And the Army, the Army has it passed the Beresina?

AIDE DE CORPS

A 3rd crossed, almost —but the bridge gave way.

BONAPARTE

I know it.

AIDE DE CORPS

And from one moment to the other.

BONAPARTE

Silence! And you say that Thitchikov—?

AIDE DE CORPS

That's his cannon approaching.

BONAPARTE

Does the sacred battalion still have men?

AIDE DE CORPS

Five hundred,—a little less.

BONAPARTE

Let them hold Thitchikov and his 30,000 men and give the Army time to pass the Beresina. By deploying them in a single line they will appear to be triple that number. Go—oh, the bridge, the bridge—I had told Eble that the trestles were not strong enough. At each instant I dread to hear the sound of thousands of unfortunate who have drowned. My God! Someone got any wine!

SPY

Here's some drops.

BONAPARTE

Thanks.

(he's going to drink and sees one of his Grenadiers dying, suffering—he brings him the gourd)

Hold, my brave fellow!

(cries of distress mingled with shouts of hurrahs from the Cossacks)

Ah! The bridge is broken.

VOICES

(outside)

The bridge, the bridge.

OTHER VOICES

The enemy! The Cossacks!

BONAPARTE

To us, boys! Outside and march. Half the Army is drowned—we must save the rest.

WOMAN

(to the Spy)

Oh from pity don't leave me here. I cannot march.

(The Spy wraps her in his cape and carries her in his arms)

SPY

Come. I still have some strength left.

BLACKOUT

ACT III

Tableau 9

(Napoléon—stick in hand followed by some soldiers, troops marching.)

MUSICIANS

(of the 1st Corps—seeing Napoléon)

The Emperor! The Emperor!

(They play "Where Could It Be Better?")

BONAPARTE

No—boys—play "Let's Stand to Salute the Empire"!

(at length the music moves off; the soldiers becomes more scattered, they fall—the snow covers them!)

CURTAIN

ACT IV

Tableau 10

The Emperor's office at the Tuileries.

(Napoléon, a Minister, Secretaries, Envoys)

BONAPARTE

(to Envoy)

A year ago all Europe marched with us. Today all Europe marches against us. I need a levee of 300,000 men; tell the Senate in my name that I am counting on it.

ENVOY

Sire, the Senate begs you to try a last effort for making peace. It is the need of France and the wish of humanity. The people also ask guarantees. Without that, it is impossible.

BONAPARTE

Gentlemen, with this language, instead of uniting us, you will divide us. Are you unaware that in a monarchy the throne and the monarch cannot be separated? What is the throne? A stick of wood covered with silk—but in the language of monarchy: I am the throne. You speak of the people; are you unaware that it is I who represent the people above all? One cannot attack me without attacking the nation itself. If there is some abuse, is this the moment to make a remonstrance when 200,000 Cossacks are ready to cross our frontiers? You ask in the name of France guarantees against power? Listen to France—she asks guarantees only against the enemy. If France knows among my marshals a general more capable of resisting foreign aggression, then name him, and I will put myself and my sword under him. Go gentlemen, and convey my orders to the Senate.

(to a Secretary)

Write: engineers will be sent on the routes in the North.

(to another Secretary)

Write: the arms manufacturers of St. Étienne Liège, and Mauberg will put at the disposition of the government.

FIRST SECRETARY

(repeating)

"…in the North."

BONAPARTE

(going to him)

They will be charged with rebuilding ancient walls which served as the ramparts of Old France—

(to another Secretary)

Write: "The German Army has just crossed our borders by the bridges at Mayence. "

SECOND SECRETARY

"…of the government."

BONAPARTE

"One Hundred Fifty Thousand rifles and 30,000 sabers not later than fifteen days from today." Give it to me.

(signing)

THIRD SECRETARY

(repeating)

"…by the bridges at Mayence."

BONAPARTE

"It will form and extend its line from Hunigue to the sands of Holland." Give it to me.

FIRST SECRETARY

"…the ancient walls which served as the ramparts of Old France."

BONAPARTE

Of Old France: to layout the forts on heights to serve as rallying points in case of retreat." Put the seal on it, gentlemen and hurry "in case of retreat."

FIRST SECRETARY

I cannot do it, Sire.

BONAPARTE

Very well.

(to another)

Sit at my desk and write. "Minister of War—the Minister of the Royal Treasury, will convey to the hands of the Minister of War."

FIRST SECRETARY

(repeating)

"…In case of retreat."

BONAPARTE

"Then do all to prepare for the destruction of the dikes and bridges which must be abandoned."

THIRD SECRETARY

(repeating)

To the Minister of War.

BONAPARTE

"The sum of thirty million francs—

MINISTER

Your Majesty knows that the Treasury has no money left.

BONAPARTE

Ah—well, then, tear it up.

(writing)

Here's a good thirty million from my privy purse.

MINISTER

From your privy purse? Your Majesty knows that these funds were destined for secret placements to assure the fate of your family in case of reversals.

BONAPARTE

(severely)

Sir, the Emperor owns nothing. The money he possesses belongs to his people, and in case of defeat he will bequeath his son and his wife to the people. Go gentlemen! Minister stay, I have instructions for you.

(displaying a map)

Three Allied Armies are readying to enter France. That of Schwarzenberg will penetrate through Switzerland. The Emperors Alexander, the King of Prussia and the Emperor of Austria follow his person—it amounts in total to 200,000 men. The second commanded by Marshal Blucher, has forced a passage at

Mannheim and pours into Lorrain with a strength of 500,000 men. The third under the orders of the Prince of Sweden, reinforced by the Russians of Voronzov and the Prussians of Bulow, after having crossed through Hanover and destroyed the Kingdom of Westphalia will be reinforced by the English under Graham and take Holland and Belgium. It is 200,000 men strong. These forces assembled there are 550,000 men which when uniting with their reserves grow to 800,000. What are the forces you can put at my disposition?

MINISTER

Eighty thousand men—a little less.

BONAPARTE

In all?

MINISTER

In all.

BONAPARTE

It's not much. But I will fight them separately. I will try not to have them three against one. I will join battle with them in the plains of Champagne at Chalons or at Beienne. Let Marshal Victor depart and have him announce my arrival to the troops. I will depart tonight. Inform the Empress that I am going to be with her after I've received the Chiefs of the National Guard.

(Enter Usher)

USHER

Sire, a man has come in with the password. He says he must speak with you immediately.

BONAPARTE

Let him come in.

(Usher exits)

(enter the Spy)

Ah! It's you! Well what's gone wrong?

SPY

Sire, your most dangerous enemies are not on the frontier.

BONAPARTE

Speak quickly.

SPY

A conspiracy has just been organized in France.

BONAPARTE

To what end?

SPY

To bring back the Bourbons.

BONAPARTE

How do you know this?

SPY

I am a member.

BONAPARTE

Who are the heads?

SPY

Here's a list.

BONAPARTE

Where are they meeting?

SPY

At the Château Lisse in Touraine.

BONAPARTE

The Bourbons! The Bourbons! They will see if ever the Bourbons reign over them! So foreign enemies and domestic enemies! Blood on the battlefield—blood in the Marketplace! It's too much at one time. Only a victory can save us. We must always conquer!

(writing)

Now, take this order to Fouché let him watch them without arresting them. I don't wish it. Leave this way—ah, here are the heads of the National Guard.

(exit Spy)

(enter the Head Guardsman)

Gentlemen, I leave with confidence. I am going to fight the enemy. I leave you with what I hold most dear—the Empress and my son. Do you swear to defend them?

HEADS

We swear it.

BONAPARTE

Letters patent confer regency on the Empress. I add to her Prince Joseph as Lt. General of the Empire. You recognize their power and will obey them?

HEADS

We swear it.

BONAPARTE

Prince de Neuchatel—is everything ready for my departure?

BERTHIER

His Majesty will take his coach whenever he wishes.

BONAPARTE

Come, let's embrace my wife and child for the last time, perhaps.

BLACKOUT

ACT IV

Tableau 11

Montereau—a height on which are found a battery of cannons firing.

(Napoléon is seated on a gun carriage. He whips his boot with a riding crop and talks to himself.)

BONAPARTE

Come on, come on Bonaparte. Save Napoléon.

(rising and running to the artillerymen)

In the streets my friends, in the streets. The Württembergers are crowded together. Too high—you aim too high.

(pointing himself)

Fire!

(One hears the cannon of the enemy responding. The whistle of bullets—some artillerymen fall.)

ARTILLERY MAN

Sire, get back.

BONAPARTE

Don't be jealous my friend—it's my old job.

ARTILLERY MAN

Sire, it's a veritable hurricane of fire. Get back.

BONAPARTE

Take it easy, boys—the bullet that will kill me hasn't been made. Ah, there's the opening in the town.

(to an Aide de Corps)

Run, sir! Have General Pajol descend on Montereau by the Melieu road. Where's the Duke of Bellune's Corps? Ah! I have them in my very hands! I have them all! Don't let them still slip between my fingers. Bellune—why hasn't he moved from the other side of the Seine?

AIDE DE CAMP

(running in)

Sire, he came too late to cross the Seine in time—he was tired. He's taken off in pursuit of the enemy.

BONAPARTE

Too late—tired! Am I tired? My soldiers are tired? No, we know better than to be tired. Run to General Château and tell him to take 2,000 cavalry to cut off the retreat.

AIDE DE CAMP

He's dead.

BONAPARTE

Château dead! He was a hero! Bellune! Bellune! They don't want to fight. They are all too rich. I've gorged them with diamonds—they must take their repose—on their lands—in their Château.

(to an Aide de Corps)

Go tell General Gérard to take command of General Bellune's corps—and tell Bellune I permit him to retire to his lands. Go—what a loss of time!

SOLDIERS

(arriving)

Long live the Emperor!

BONAPARTE

(looking with his telescope)

What's going on? Why isn't General Guyon with his Chasseurs and his artillery?

AIDE DE CAMP

The enemy surprised him and captured his artillery.

BONAPARTE

His artillery? He let them take his artillery? Come on—why aren't they firing more now?

ARTILLERY MAN

(crossing)

Munitions. Comrades have you any munitions?

BONAPARTE

Who sent you?

ARTILLERY MAN

General Digeon.

BONAPARTE

What—Digeon? Digeon—he too lacks munitions? Why didn't he take his precautions? Does he believe my battles are skirmishes involving five hundred cannon shells? Hey! Hey! One of my best Generals of artillery. Go, go—it's too late. Let the enemy army escape for the tenth time rather than for the tenth time I hold him up by the waist.

(to a staff messenger)

Where are you from?

MESSENGER

From the forest of Fontainebleau.

BONAPARTE

Montbrun protects it, I hope?

MESSENGER

He's been obliged to abandon it to the Cossacks.

BONAPARTE

Still a useless victory—more blood wasted. And all this because Bellune didn't proceed fast enough. Tired! Tired! Tired! And I—do I go in a carriage? Ah, I'll try Digeon by a court-martial and bad luck to him.

GENERAL SORBIER

Sire, you know that Digeon is a brave man.

BONAPARTE

Yes, I know it! It is just because I know it that: he is more capable. What an example to the others! General, there are some examples that are worse than crimes.

GENERAL SORBIER

Do you recall his wonderful charge at Champ-Aubert, his two horses killed at Montmerail—his clothes riddled with shot at Nanges?

BONAPARTE

Yes, yes—let's not speak of it any more.

(A new messenger appears with a letter.)

Murat, too. Murat to whom I ought to be sacred. Murat my brother-in-law—he declares against me. Well—the army of Lyons has become useless.

AIDE DE CAMP

A courier.

BONAPARTE

From whom?

COURIER

The Duke of Trévise.

BONAPARTE

Well—he pursued the enemy to Château-Thierry, right? And he will take him between there and Soissons.

COURIER

Soissons has surrendered.

BONAPARTE

Who is the General commanding there?

COURIER

General Moreau.

BONAPARTE

That name has always brought me misfortune. Still there's a plan to change the campaign. The enemy is advancing on Paris by Villers-Cotterêts and Nanteuil?

COURIER

It's at Dammartin.

BONAPARTE

Ten leagues from my capital! Not an instant to lose to save it. Come, gentlemen. Ah, we'll pay him dearly for his audacity. He adventures deep into our provinces and leaves us behind to shut off his retreat. From the beginning of this campaign I've dreamed of this maneuver. Withdraw from all the cities—let the troops abandon them and march on Paris. Send this order by messengers. If Paris holds only two days we will take them between two fires.

ALL

A courier from Paris! A courier from Paris!

BONAPARTE

What do you bring me?

COURIER

A letter from Mr. Lavellette.

BONAPARTE

"Sire, your presence is necessary in Paris on which the enemy marches from all sides. If you don't want the capital to be given up to the enemy, there is not a moment to lose." Yes, I'm worth more than an army in the midst of them. My presence will excite my brave Parisians' Marshal! I leave you in the command of the troops. March to Fontainebleau. Forward orders to Ragusa and Trévise—that they hasten and march on Paris. I must be in my Capital before this evening. Oh, what a war! Let them march without delay, double—triple time. We will rally all our cannons in Montmartre.

BLACKOUT

ACT IV

Tableau 12

A room (salon) in the Faubourg St. Germaine.

MARQUIS

Ah, good evening Baron—what news?

BARON

Bad! Bonaparte has beaten the Prussians at Champs-Aubert and at Montmirail.

MARQUIS

It is certain?

BARON

Wait—ask the Vicomte!

VICOMTE

Ah, my dear, it's very bad. The allies are in full retreat. Pursued at saber point to Château Thierry. The people are rising and arming with Prussian muskets with which the roads are covered—if Soissons holds everything is lost.

MARQUIS

Do you know if the allied sovereigns have received our letters in time?

BARON

They were sent by a trusty man.

VICOMTE

Peace is not to be feared then?

MARQUIS

No—the conditions which they impose on him are not accept-
able. It must seem he wants war. What is that?

BARON

What?

MARQUIS

That noise!

BARON

(at the window)

What is it, my brave?

A MAN

(in the street)

Ten thousand Russian prisoners passing on the boulevard. Come
see them!

CRIER

Here's the latest news! Bulletin of a great victory won by the
Emperor Napoléon at Montmirail and at Champ Aubert.

MARQUIS

Come on!

(throwing himself in an armchair)

What is to be done?

BARON

He won't last. This man beats them wherever he finds them but it can't last much longer. Have you received letters from the Comte d'Artois?

VICOMTE

Yes. He is at Franche-Comté with the Russians.

MARQUIS

And his son?

VICOMTE

The Duke d'Angoulême is with the English in the Midi. The Duke de Berry is in Jersey. All's well there.

BARON

But it must be made known to the allied sovereigns.

ALL

Without doubt, without doubt.

MARQUIS

Have you seen the proclamation of Louis XVIII dated from Hartwell? Very fine—pardons—jobs—

VICOMTE

Well—but it is impossible that Bonaparte with his 40,000 men can still resist.

MARQUIS

But the allies think he has more men.

BARON

They must be informed of his weakness.

ALL

For certain.

VICOMTE

But there must be a trusty man who's not afraid to pass through French ranks. As for Paris, there's nothing to fear—the Police are for us.

MARQUIS

I will go if you wish it.

BARON

You?

VICOMTE

You?

MARQUIS

Yes. If I'm shot you will say to my mother, "He died worthy of you—worthy of his father—he died for the legitimate princes."

BARON

How will you get through?

MARQUIS

In livery. I will pretend to belong to some General. But a passport?

VICOMTE

I have three or four in blank that the Prefecture has given me in case of need.

MARQUIS

Well—quickly then—there's no time to lose. Give me the letters.

(calling)

Germaine!

GERMAINE

(Entering)

Sir?

MARQUIS

Get me one of your livery and go find a post horse. You will wait for me at the corner of the Rue St. Honoré and the Rue Rohan. I will go at full gallop until Villers-Cotterêts. From there, I'll go on foot. Fine!—letters from the Count D'Artois and the Duke de Berry. You, see here the Duke of—

ALL

Yes, yes.

MARQUIS

Don't tell my mother where I am. She loves her King well—but she loves her son more.

ALL

Goodbye, goodbye, my brave Marquis!

VICOMTE

Good luck in the issue.

BARON

Bon voyage, my friend.

MARQUIS

Come—escort me.

BLACKOUT

ACT IV

Tableau 13

A street in Paris.

> *(Labredèche, workers—people, etc.)*

WORKER

Give us muskets! Muskets! We don't ask more than to fight! Hide the wealth—that's okay—but give us arms while the Prussians are in Montmartre!

ALL

Yes. Arms! Arms!

ANOTHER WORKER

Tell the others. I'm back from the Arsenal—I've got shells.

WORKER

Muskets then, muskets!

FIRST WORKER

You've got to go to town to get muskets.

AN ARMOURER

(opening his shop)

Hold on, my braves—I—I've got muskets—rifles, hunting rifles, carbines. Take—take them all—leave only one for me.

WORKERS

Ah! Bravo! Bravo!

LABREDÈCHE

Things are heating up, heating up.

FIRST WORKER

Damnation! There's sand in these cartridges!

ALL

Sand?

FIRST WORKER

In this one at least.

STUDENT

Comrade, we've been given bullets which have no caliber and cartridges filled with ashes.

WORKERS

We are betrayed! We've been sold out! To the Arsenal! To the Arsenal!

(Some students pass at the rear aiming their weapons and carrying bullets)

WORKERS

Long live the Polytechnic Institute!

LABREDÈCHE

What little fops! If I had told them of my two brothers who died in Russia.

ALL

To Montmartre, to Montmartre.

FIRST WORKER

(to Labredèche)

Are you coming with us to Montmartre?

LABREDÈCHE

No, my braves, no. I'm going to stay here to work. Comrades.

FIRST WORKER

Ah so! Perhaps you're afraid?

LABREDÈCHE

Me—afraid? Not at all! I don't have a musket.

ARMONO

Well—here's one—my brave.

FIRST WORKER

Put ammo in your pockets and come.

LABREDÈCHE

Right, right my friend, give me the pleasure of giving me a light from your cigar. It's so I can blow up like a magazine!

FIRST WORKER

Ah, bah!

LABREDÈCHE

It's not for me—it's for the citizens so I can wound others in blowing up.

POLICE AGENT

Assemblies are forbidden.

SECOND WORKER

By God—if we assemble it's to fight.

SOME PEOPLE

(mixing with them)

But you see indeed you've been betrayed. Come on, believe us, don't get yourselves killed.

FIRST WORKER

(returning)

My friends, they don't wish us to leave this barricade. We are more than 10,000 armies. It's treason! Damnation!

WORKERS

Force the gates.

WOMAN

Sound the Tocsin.

ALL

Ah, yes—the tocsin.

(prolonged shouts—A messenger on horseback)

WORKER

What news? What news?

MESSENGER

The Emperor! The Emperor! He's returning by direction of Fontainebleau—he's not six leagues from here! Courage! Courage!

WORKER

We've got that—if someone will lead us. Ah, there's the tocsin. The Emperor's returning—are you sure?

ANOTHER

He is at the Fontainebleau barricade.

ANOTHER

They say he came in disguise.

ANOTHER

The Empress left with the King of Rome.

(noise)

What's that?

ANOTHER

Stop—stop—a man's wearing the white cockade.

MAN

(trying to escape)

My friends, my friends.

FIRST WORKER

Dog! Brigand! So you'd bring us back the Bourbons!

MAN

My friends, I beg you.

FIRST WORKER

Go on—you're not worth a bullet. To Montmartre my friends to Montmartre.

SECOND WORKER

(to Labredèche)

Well, aren't you coming?

LABREDÈCHE

You see I'm bringing up the rear, up the rear, up the rear.

WORKER

(running after those who have just left)

Hey, wait, wait, you there—have you got a musket—cartridges?

LABREDÈCHE

My friend, my friend, this is your business. I've just come from the barricades where I was fighting like a madman. Here's what's left of my 300 cartridges—and here's a musket I captured.

WORKER

Thanks, but you?

(taking the musket)

LABREDÈCHE

I am charged with a dangerous and important mission.

WORKER

Go, good luck!

LABREDÈCHE

And you, too.

(the Worker goes)

Let's see this cockade. In fact it's not as pretty as the tricolor but it's the color of legitimacy. Put legitimacy in one pocket, usurpation in the other—God will decide the question. I'm not going to mix with it any more—it's too complicated.

BLACKOUT

ACT IV

Tableau 14

A Hall in the Fontainebleau Palace.

BONAPARTE

(rushing into the apartment)

Horses! Horses!

RUSTAN

They've been harnessed to the carriage, Sire.

BONAPARTE

Fifteen leagues! Fifteen leagues from Fontainebleau to Paris—I need three hours—my brave Parisians, how they defend themselves!

DOMESTIC

The horses are ready.

BONAPARTE

Let's go.

ANOTHER DOMESTIC

An envoy from the Duke of Vicenza.

BONAPARTE

Convoy to Paris.

(to the Envoy)

What's wrong, sir?

ENVOY

Paris is taken, Sire.

BONAPARTE

What do you say? Paris is taken? That cannot be.

ENVOY

The Capitulation was signed at two o'clock in the morning and at this moment the Allies are entering into the Capital.

BONAPARTE

Paris surrendered! And soon the columns that I led from Champagne will empty into Sens.

ENVOY

And into Essonne. You can see from here the advance guard of the troops leaving Paris.

BONAPARTE

Paris surrendered! Are you certain?

ENVOY

Ask the Dukes of Ragusa and Trévise.

(The Dukes enter)

BONAPARTE

Oh, Ragusa, Ragusa, is it true that you have surrendered Paris?

RAGUSA

An order from Prince Joseph ordered me to negotiate.

BONAPARTE

And the Empress—and my child? You will answer to me, Marshal, for my child!

RAGUSA

Their Majesties have retired to the Loire with the Ministers.

BONAPARTE

How many men do you bring me, gentlemen?

RAGUSA

I bring nine thousand.

TRÉVISE

I bring six thousand.

BONAPARTE

(to Ney)

Prince, where are the troops that you command?

NEY

Sire, they rejoin the general quarters.

BONAPARTE

How many men? Paris lost.

NEY

Ten thousand.

BONAPARTE

And you, gentlemen?

DUKE OF TARENTO & THE PRINCE OF NEU-
CHATEL

Fifteen thousand—a little less.

BONAPARTE

Then I still have 40,000 men at hand?

NEY

Yes, but discouraged, tired—

BONAPARTE

What are you saying, Prince?

(showing himself at the window)

SOLDIERS

Long live the Emperor—long live the Emperor! To Paris! To
Paris! March on Paris!

BONAPARTE

(returning)

You hear! They are not tired gentlemen! Duke of Ragusa—place
your general quarters at Essonne. You will be my advance guard.

RAGUSA

Sire, it's a great responsibility.

BONAPARTE

If I knew a man more sure than you, old Comrade, it is to him that I would confide your Emperor. I will be tranquil Marmont so long as you watch over me. Marshal Trévise you will establish your camp at Menney. Those who come from Paris will rally behind your line. Those arriving from Champagne will take a position in between on the side of Fontainebleau. The baggage train and main park will be directed on Orleans. Give your orders.

DUKE OF TARENTO

(in a half voice)

He's going to march on Paris and our wives and children are hostages there. When will you finish?

BONAPARTE

(turning)

Well—you've heard me, gentlemen.

VOICE

(in the antechamber)

The Duke of Vicenza, the Duke of Vicenza.

TARENTO

Caulaincourt!

BONAPARTE

Caulaincourt!

DUKE OF TARENTO

What news? What's wrong, Duke? Well—Paris?

CAULAINCOURT

Surrendered.

BONAPARTE

The allies?

CAULAINCOURT

They entered this morning.

BONAPARTE

Well, gentlemen, I think I have some business with the Duke of Vicenza. Go give your orders. Go, go.

(they leave)

What is it Caulaincourt?—speak—

CAULAINCOURT

Sire, the Senate has proclaimed the dethronement—

BONAPARTE

Of whom?

CAULAINCOURT

Of the Emperor Napoléon.

BONAPARTE

My dethronement—mine? The Senate? Ah, the fools! Have you seen the Allied sovereigns?

CAULAINCOURT

All.

BONAPARTE

And Alexander?

CAULAINCOURT

Yes.

BONAPARTE

Well—what do they say? What are the conditions they impose on me? Speak quickly—can't you see I'm on fire?

CAULAINCOURT

They are violent partisans of the Bourbons.

BONAPARTE

The Bourbons! The Bourbons! It's I who am Emperor. They have recognized me as such. They have called me their brother— the Bourbons—it's impossible!

CAULAINCOURT

Sire, there may yet be a way to conserve the throne in Your Majesty's favor. It's to abdicate in favor of the King of Rome with regency in the Empress.

BONAPARTE

But, Duke, I have here 40,000 men. The enemy which has just lost at least 12,000 men in the streets of Paris. Their generals are dispersed in hotels—in eight days I can march a 100,000 men on the Capital!

CAULAINCOURT

Sire, there's a weariness of war.

BONAPARTE

The Parisians will rally to the sounds of my cannons.

CAULAINCOURT

Sire, cries of long live the King and long live the Bourbons were proffered yesterday in the streets—many windows were hung with white flags—Sire, in the name of heaven—it costs me— Sire, abdicate in favor of the King of Rome.

BONAPARTE

Eh! What do my old generals say?

(turning towards center)

Marshals—enter—all enter—where is Ragusa?

A MARSHAL

With the avant-garde.

BONAPARTE

Do you know what is being proposed to me? An abdication in favor of the King of Rome.

MARSHAL

And do you think the allied sovereigns will be content with that?

BONAPARTE

Content with it?

MARSHAL

Really, sire.

BONAPARTE

Well?

MARSHAL

You must abdicate; then the King of Rome can be recognized. If they won't recognize the King of Rome, we will tell you: "Sire, we are ready to march."

BONAPARTE

Ah—then it's your advice, too? You want peace? Have it, then. You don't know how many shames and dangers will attend you on your feather beds . Some years of this peace will make you pay more dearly for this harvest than the greatest number in the most desperate war. All right.

(he writes)

"The powers having proclaimed that the Emperor Napoléon is the sole obstacle to the re-establishment of peace in Europe, the Emperor Napoléon faithful to his oath declares that he is ready to descend the throne. To leave France and even forgo life for the good of his country—inseparable from the rights of his son and of the regency of the Empress and for the maintenance of the laws of the Empire. Done at our Palace of Fontainebleau, 5 April 1814. Napoléon." Wait gentlemen—this is indeed my signature! You must recognize it—it is on all your deeds as Marshals and Princes—go, Duke, and take them this scrap of paper. It's the ruination of a beautiful throne. Oh, if I had done to them as they have done to me. Go gentlemen and leave me alone.

(to Caulaincourt)

Tarento and Trévise will accompany you.

(they leave)

(taking a medal)

Ah, my son, my child—for you. For you—yes. I can submit to anything, support anything. Those men that I have created from myself, whose attire I have emblazoned. Only my soldiers remain faithful and devoted to me—I must thank them.

(calling)

Secretary!

SECRETARY

(entering)

Sire!

BONAPARTE

Write: "The Emperor thanks the army for the attachment it has shown him. Because it recognizes that France is in him and not in the masses of stones, and streets and mud that we call the Capital. The Senate is permitted to dispose of the Government of France; it has forgotten that it owes a duty to the Emperor not to abuse that power. So long as fortune was favorable to him the Senate was faithful. If the Emperor scorned these men as they have reproached him now—the world can see today that he had reasons which motivated his scorn. He held the dignity of the nation; the nation alone could deprive him of it. He has always"—

(The Duke of Vicenza enters)

What's wrong, Vicenza, and why haven't you gone?

CAULAINCOURT

I met a courier as I was getting into my carriage, and he brought me this new dispatch. Read—

BONAPARTE

A formal abdication ready-made for me—and for my son. Abdicate for my son? Never!

CAULAINCOURT

Sire, Louis XVIII has been proclaimed King.

BONAPARTE

Who cares? Didn't you hear just now that my Marshals told me if it was exacted that I abdicate for my son, they were ready to march on Paris? Ah, if they are insensible to affronts to their

Emperor, they at least will avenge their old Comrade. Duke—call them! In six hours we will be before Paris.

CAULAINCOURT

There's no one in the antechamber.

BONAPARTE

Tell the usher to call them.

CAULAINCOURT

(to an usher)

Santini—call the Marshals. What? There aren't any?

BONAPARTE

(returning)

What did he say? This man is mistaken. I called my Marshals.

CAULAINCOURT

Sire, they took their horses just now and left.

BONAPARTE

To go where?

CAULAINCOURT

They took the road to Paris.

(after a silence)

Oh—I am very—you see, Sire—they too abandon you.

BONAPARTE

Never mind! Ragusa remains to me. Ragusa and I will suffer with the army and the army will suffer with us. Duke!

GOUGARD

(entering)

Sire, Sire. All the road to Fontainebleau is open. The Duke of Ragusa has gone over to the enemy with the 10,000 men he commanded.

BONAPARTE

He, too! The ingrate! Ragusa! The child I raised in my tent. The one I told to watch when I slept. He's a traitor! Oh, there will be many more misfortunes for me! Leave me alone gentlemen.

CAULAINCOURT

Sire.

BONAPARTE

Leave me alone, I beg you.

GOUGARD

Sire, Fontainebleau is open from the direction of Paris. What orders do you give?

BONAPARTE

None.

(They leave.)

BONAPARTE

Ah, it's an infamous abandonment. I see it clearly. The allies fear me as much as a general for my son then as Emperor of France. My child—my poor child! It was for him that I amassed crowns. And it is I who take it from him. So long as I live, they will tremble. Oh what an idea! Yes! My death—my son is the legitimate heir of my throne. In the depth of my fall I have nothing to fear. The sovereigns would be ashamed to rob an orphan. How happy I would have been to have taken Cabanis' poison. It's the same he prepared for Condorcet.

(He takes something precipitously from his neck and opens a little packet which he puts in a glass)

They will say that I lack courage to support my life—that death is a flight. Who cares what they say? Don't I know the truth?

(cutting his hair and putting it in a paper)

For my son—come, come, it's only a toast to his fortune.

(he drinks)

Goodbye my son! Goodbye France.

(he falls into his chair, head on his hands)

> SPY

(at the door)

What's he done?

> BONAPARTE

Ah, there's the poison. Well, Cabanis told me that this poison was as fast as thought—ah, after four years of carrying it around it will be weak. It's only strong enough to make me suffer—not to kill me—ah.

> SPY

(entering)

No doubt—the Emperor is poisoned. Sire.

> BONAPARTE

Silence!

> SPY

Help, help, the Emperor is dying. Ruston! Ruston! The Wretch. He also has abandoned him. Constant! Nobody!

(he rings)

Ah, if blood was an antidote against the poison—help! Help!

BONAPARTE

There's no need! Poison is like bullets. Death doesn't want me.

CAULAINCOURT

(entering)

What's wrong?

SPY

Ah, Duke, where is Doctor Ivan?

CAULAINCOURT

Leaving by horse right now. But what's wrong with the Emperor?

SPY

He's—

BONAPARTE

Silence—on your head!

(to Caulaincourt)

Nothing, Duke—an indisposition.

(aside)

God doesn't wish it.

CAULAINCOURT

How pale Your Majesty is.

BONAPARTE

Duke—what residence is accorded to me if I abdicate?

CAULAINCOURT

Corfu, Corsica, or the Island of Elba.

BONAPARTE

I choose the Island of Elba. Do they permit me to take someone from my household or from my army?

CAULAINCOURT

Four hundred Grenadiers and the people from your household that you designate. If Your Majesty agrees—Bertrand, Drouot, and Cambronne ask the favor of following you.

BONAPARTE

They who never asked anything during the height of my fortune! Posterity will reward the courtiers of misfortune.

(goes to the writing table and writes)

"The allied powers having proclaimed that the Emperor Napoléon is the sole obstacle to the reestablishment of peace in Europe, the Emperor Napoléon, faithful to his oath, declares that he renounces for him and his children the Thrones of France and Italy, and that there is no sacrifice, not even of his life that he will not be ready to make for the interests of France—April 6, 1814"—are you satisfied, Duke?

CAULAINCOURT

I have only one grace to ask of you!

BONAPARTE

What?

CAULAINCOURT

That Your Majesty will permit me to accompany him to the Island of Elba.

BONAPARTE

You, Caulaincourt? That cannot be.

CAULAINCOURT

Sire?

BONAPARTE

Return to Paris. Your presence is awaited with impatience.

(to an usher)

Go tell General Petit to put his soldiers under arms in the Great Courtyard. I wish to say goodbye to my braves for the last time. Caulaincourt, France will regret me! And all those who have take part in my ruin will be cursed by her. Adieu, Caulaincourt. Adieu.

CAULAINCOURT

(kissing his hand)

Adieu, Sire.

(Caulaincourt leaves center. Napoléon takes his hat from a table—hesitates a moment thoughtfully, then leaves stage left.)

BLACKOUT

ACT IV

Tableau 15

The Whitehouse Court at Fontainebleau.

LORRAIN

Speak then, hey—old ones! They say that we're to be sent to our respective homes. You aren't going—right?

ALL THE SOLDIERS

No! No!

LORRAIN

Me neither—no more. They say the Emperor is no longer Emperor—they've lied—right?

SOLDIERS

Yes—yes.

LORRAIN

And they cannot take him from us while we still have four men to make him a square—right?

SOLDIERS

We'll all die.

LORRAIN

(striking his musket)

Sacred rascal! Let them come on now.

(Enter General Petit.)

PETIT

Soldiers—to your arms.

SOLDIERS

The Emperor! The Emperor! The Emperor!

(Napoléon appears at the center—on the grand staircase)

SOLDIERS

Long live the Emperor! To Paris—to Paris!

(Napoléon motions for silence)

SOLDIERS

Hush—silence! He is going to speak.

BONAPARTE

Soldiers of my old guard! I bid you farewell. For twenty years I have found you constant on the road to honor and glory—in these last times as in those of our prosperity, you've never ceased to be models of fidelity and bravery. With men such as you, our cause was not lost—but the war was interminable—it had become a civil war and France was only becoming most unfortunate. I have, therefore, sacrificed the interests of all of us to those of the country. I am leaving. You, my friends, continue to serve France. France's happiness was my unique thought. It will always be the object of my wishes. Don't complain about my fate. If I have consented to survive, it's to further serve your glory. I intend to write about the great things we have done together! Adieu, my boys—I would press you all to my heart—let me embrace at least your flags.

(General Petit grabs the Eagle and presents it to Napoléon who embraces it.)

BONAPARTE

Adieu, one more time, very old companions! May this kiss enter your hearts.

CURTAIN

ACT V

Tableau 16

The Ministry of War—the Antechamber of the Minister—Audience day.

(Two Ushers—Solicitors enter)

USHER

Number four.

SOLICITOR

That's me.

LABREDÈCHE

(entering)

Good day, my friends, good day.

USHER

Sir?

LABREDÈCHE

What—you don't recognize me?

USHER

Ah, isn't it the gentleman whose father was shot by firing squad?

LABREDÈCHE

Yes, my friend. Well—it is as usual. And I am soliciting you know—you ought to know it—for each day for eight months I've repeated it at public audience—ah—you've kept my number haven't you?

USHER

You always come on the side of the regular customer.

LABREDÈCHE

Tell your friends and I am your friend—your true friend— Number 9—? Where is it?

USHER

Number 4 has just gone in.

LABREDÈCHE

Bravo! The day when I shall obtain the pension which is so due to me, as the sole and unique heir of a family which has sacrificed itself for the good old cause—I will not forget—my brave fellow—all that you have done for me. Is that today's journal you have there?

USHER

Yes—Tuesday, February 28, 1815.

OLD SOLDIER

(entering)

Will you give me a number, please?

USHER

(to his usher friend)

Would you see if there are any numbers left?

SECOND USHER

Here's number 18.

OLD SOLDIER

My turn will be long in coming my friend. Can't you find one a little closer in. You see we are not even 7 or 8.

SECOND USHER

No.

OLD SOLDIER

There's only time for two an hour. The public audience will be over before my number comes up. And perhaps even today his Excellency—

USHER

Well, you will return next Tuesday.

OLD SOLDIER

(sitting)

Yes, I'll be here if I haven't died of hunger.

LABREDÈCHE

(to 1st Usher)

I've already seen this mug before.

USHER

He's a solicitor.

LABREDÈCHE

The antechambers are encumbered with these types—is there anything in the journal?

USHER

"The King attended Mass in his apartments."

LABREDÈCHE

Ah! So much the better! So much the better!

USHER

"The Minister of War worked with His Majesty!"

LABREDÈCHE

Perhaps, he has already put my petition before the eyes of the son of St. Louis.

(raising his voice)

This minister of yours is a great man. And I say this though he cannot hear me, I am not a flatterer.

USHER

(reading)

The Marquis of Feuillade his just been named colonel of the 3rd Horse Regiment.

OLD SOLDIER

Colonel?—a child.

LABREDÈCHE

He's a devoted man, a pure monarchist without doubt who has acquired some rights and who like me has been a victim.

USHER

Yes, yes. His father had a post—raised in the home of Louis XVI. He had the goblet or garde-robe—I don't know much.

LABREDÈCHE

That's right. And do they say his regiment will take his name?

OLD SOLDIER

(aside, sourly)

Under the Emperor it was called "The Intrepid".

SECOND USHER

(calling)

Number 6.

LABREDÈCHE

He called number 6, right? My turn approaches, is there anything else?

USHER

"His Majesty has named chevaliers of the Legion of Honor—M. LeConte de Formont—Captain of the Hunt. His Highness Monsieur Royale—M. Le Marquis de Lartigues, 3rd Valet de Chamber to his Highness, Royal Lord the Duke of Berry, Monsieur de—

(the old soldier tears his ribbon)

My word this is too long—"His Eminence, the Archbishop of Toulouse has been received in a private audience with His Majesty."

SECOND USHER

(calling)

Number 7.

USHER

Pardon, I must leave you.

LABREDÈCHE

Don't trouble yourself, my friend, don't trouble yourself.

(going to the old soldier)

Sir, are you looking for a place or a pension.

OLD SOLDIER

Neither the one nor the other. I ask for active duty.

LABREDÈCHE

It's difficult, difficult at this time.

OLD SOLDIER

I have twenty years of service.

LABREDÈCHE

That's why. It's other people's turn. And you were?

OLD SOLDIER

Captain.

LABREDÈCHE

Captain. You understand that's a grade which corresponds to the son of a family. We have no more war. We need young men who know how to uphold our old reputation for gallantry and lightness in the salons—who can open a ball, sing a romance, beat a drum. Besides, you were serving the tyrant.

OLD SOLDIER

The tyrant?

LABREDÈCHE

Listen, the former government did me a lot of mischief which gives me the right—besides I've never flattered it—when the Corsican ogre was on the throne I always called him Bonaparte.

SECOND USHER

Number 9.

LABREDÈCHE

Here I am. Here I am.

(He glides into the Ministry.)

OLD SOLDIER

Called him—?

(take the journal)

"News arrived from the Isle of Elba announces that its sovereign appears to have no taste for military exercises. Since his arrival, he has not reviewed the 600 men who followed him. He's occupied constantly with botany. We are assured that most of the soldiers around him ask to return to France". Why am I not there?

(Enter Feuillade as Colonel)

MARQUIS

Can I speak to his Excellency?

USHER

But I don't know if his Excellency can at this moment.

MARQUIS

His Excellency always has time for me. I am the Marquis de la Feuillade who's just been named Colonel.

USHER

Ah! Pardon. His Excellency—

MARQUIS

Is he with someone?

USHER

No, no—it's not someone. I am going to announce you.

(opening the door)

The Marquis de la Feuillade.

MINISTER

(from his apartment, to Labredèche who leaves in retreat)

Right. Right—write to His Majesty. You have rights to his favors—but on the civil list. Try to procure certificates that your mother died on the scaffold and that your father was killed by firing squad. And then we shall see.

LABREDÈCHE

Your Excellency will not forget the persecutions of which I have been the victim under the usurper?

MINISTER

No, no.

LABREDÈCHE

Your lordship will indeed—

(the door is shut in his face)

He's right—I will ask the King himself—the August son of Saint Louis will not refuse that justice it's been waiting for to the last heir of a family which has sacrificed itself entirely to his dynasty. Goodbye my friend until next Tuesday.

USHER

M'lord's carriage.

OLD SOLDIER

Come, another eight days wasted. Oh, I must speak to him. He will listen to me if I have to stop him by force.

MINISTER

(entering with the Marquis)

But it was only justice my young friend! I am enchanted to have done this for you. You understand I'd prefer to make you Marshal right away—but that would cause an outcry. Later, when you've been three months in garrison.

OLD SOLDIER

Sir—

MINISTER

(looking at him over his shoulder)

Well?

OLD SOLDIER

I am an old soldier. I've twenty years of service. I've been discharged without a pension.

MINISTER

The hours of audience is over. Come back in eight days.

OLD SOLDIER

But it's been two months, man. I've come each Tuesday and it's been impossible for me to see Your Excellency.

MINISTER

It's not my fault.

OLD SOLDIER

Sire, I've been in every campaign from the Revolution to the Empire.

MINISTER

And you ask for service. You are lucky not to be exiled.

OLD SOLDIER

Exiled for having served my country?

MINISTER

No—for having served the Jacobins and the Usurper.

OLD SOLDIER

Sir, there was at least some danger run in those times and consequently some honor.

MINISTER

Well—go ask compensation from those you have served.

OLD SOLDIER

Are these the promises that they made us on the King's return?

MINISTER

If it comes to His Majesty having to render an account of his conduct to such as you—

OLD SOLDIER

Finish, Mr. Minister—

MINISTER

Come on, come on, I have no time to listen to you.

OLD SOLDIER

You will listen to me still—

(To Feuillade who puts his hand on his sword)

Oh! Leave your sword where it is young man. It looks good there.

(to Minister)

You will listen to me for I speak for 60,000 brave men who, like me, are dying of hunger. You've done much wrong to France, in a year-more than our enemies dared hope—but take care. One doesn't try, with impunity, to debase a nation, and you have attempted to do that. You have squandered on spies and valets this cross that we dare no longer wear. From fear of being identified with them. Curse on you! You have substituted for patriots people who don't even know their country. Born in foreign lands, and who won't know how to defend it from foreign enemies. Curse on you! You have de-baptised our victories, overturned our triumphal arches, replaced Kléber and Desaix with Cadoudal and Pichegru. Curse on you! But our time is not far off when you with all your tears will pay for our tears. It won't be enough! For we will want blood. Curse—curse on you! Go, go, now.

MINISTER

Gendarmes, arrest this man.

OLD SOLDIER

At least there I'll get some bread.

BLACKOUT

ACT V

Tableau 17

Island of Elba. Porto Ferraro—Sunday, February 26, 1815—in sight, the Brig Inconstant.

BONAPARTE

Well, my old veteran, have you nothing to say?

LORRAIN

One doesn't speak under arms.

BONAPARTE

Ah! Ah! You are severe on the regulations.

LORRAIN

It's almost twenty years—it was at Toulon—that the Duke—I don't recall his ducal name—Junot then, made me guard the camp for having sung—"Oh, the sad situation." You were only commander of artillery and, I, a simple conscript—we've made our way since that time.

BONAPARTE

Well, I relieve you of your regulations. Are you bored here? Look—

LORRAIN

Fastidiously.

BONAPARTE

Do you want to return to France?

LORRAIN

With you?

BONAPARTE

With me, you know, it is impossible. Without me?

LORRAIN

Without you—no.

BONAPARTE

And do you believe that your comrades think as you do?

LORRAIN

All.

BONAPARTE

You still have relatives in France?

LORRAIN

A child isn't a closer relation to his father—and sacred rascal—you are our father—to us, or I know nothing. I believe that I even have some place an old mother—it's less than 14 years since I received this news. I was in Italy. Beautiful country by the Gods! Not too hot, not too cold and some refreshing victories. There was her letter. I had it read to me twenty-times. You know I cannot read myself. As to that, since Marengo I haven't heard of the old lady. She may have written poste restante to Vienna or Moscow—but we went so quickly we hadn't time to go to the Post Office. I don't know where she's established her camp now—but so long as the good God sends her her ration of bread and a little heat in her oven, she'll be all right. She'll be a good woman. Ah—let's not speak of that—let's not speak of that.

BONAPARTE

We have a good view at the port today.

LORRAIN

Yes, yes—that's always pleasant. Ah, I admit a need for the taste. Sire, I wasn't pleased with you.

BONAPARTE

Bah!

LORRAIN

Ah, good, I said—he's back in his garden again, digging a grafting. Sacred Rascal! Can one forget like that what one owes oneself? When one has been something before!

BONAPARTE

Ah! You say that....

(turning)

Where is this ship from? Perhaps it comes from France.

LORRAIN

Yes, a smuggler from Livorno, some fisherman from La Spezia but from France?

(he turns to see if they're coming near—then interrupting himself)

What's up?

BONAPARTE

Wait, wait—it's a friend, I believe.

SPY

Toulon and Liberty.

BONAPARTE

(to Lorrain)

Yes. Don't let anybody approach. I have to speak to this man.

(to Spy)

It's you.

SPY

Yes, Sire.

BONAPARTE

Where are you coming from?

SPY

From France.

BONAPARTE

Directly?

SPY

No—by way of Milan and La Spezia.

BONAPARTE

Who did you see in Paris?

SPY

Regnault and….

(whispers)

BONAPARTE

What have they given you for me?

SPY

Nothing. They are afraid that I wouldn't take it and—

BONAPARTE

Admit they've forgotten me like the others.

SPY

Not more than the others.

BONAPARTE

They still think of me in France?

SPY

Always.

BONAPARTE

They have spread so many fables and lies about me. Either they say that I am crazy or that I am sick. They pretend they intend to transport me to St. Helena. I don't recommend it to them. I have supplies for six months, some cannons and men to defend me. The Kings wouldn't wish to be so dishonored. They know quite well that in two years the climate would kill me—how are things in France under the Bourbons?

SPY

Sire, they haven't yet realized the hope of the French—each day the number of malcontents increases.

BONAPARTE

(warming by degrees)

I believed when I abdicated that the Bourbons, instructed and corrected by their misfortune, wouldn't fall back into the faults which caused them to lose in '89. I hoped that the King would govern well. It was the only way to escape the Cossacks. Since they have set foot in France, they've done nothing but stupidities. Their treaty of April 23, made me profoundly indignant. With a stroke of a pen, they've deprived France of Belgium—the Borders of France—it's the Rhine. It's Talleyrand who made them commit this infamy. Peace is easy on these conditions. Just give them money. If I'd been willing like they are to sign a ruinous shameful treaty, they wouldn't be sitting on my throne. But I'd have preferred to cut off my hand. I prefer to renounce the throne than to preserve it at the expense of my glory or the honor of France. My enemies said that I didn't want peace. They portrayed me as a miserable fool, avid for blood and carnage—but the world will learn the truth—they will learn on whose side was the desire to spill blood. If I had been possessed by the fury of war, I would have retired with my army to the Loire and savor at my ease mountain warfare. They offered me Italy as the price of my abdication—I refused it. When one reigns in France, one doesn't need to reign elsewhere.

(a pause)

Are my generals going to the Court? They must cut a sad figure.

SPY

They are irritated to see émigrés preferred to them—men who've never heard the noise of a cannon.

BONAPARTE

The émigrés' area always the same. So long as it is a question of making a pretty leg in the new antechamber. I always had more than I wanted. When it was a question of showing manliness, they escaped like—. I made a big mistake in recalling to France this anti-national race. What do my soldiers say?

SPY

They say that they revere the Little Corporal—and when they are forced to cry—long live the King—they add in a whisper—"Of Rome".

BONAPARTE

They still love me! What do they say about my defeats—I mean our misfortunes?

SPY

They say France has been betrayed.

BONAPARTE

They're right! Without the infamous defection of the Duke of __. I will never do him the honor of pronouncing his name. The allies were lost. Totally lost. Not one would have escaped. They would have had their 29th Bulletin. The Marshal is a wretch! He's scarred forever. He lost his country and sold his prince—all his blood would not suffice to expiate the evil he has done France. It's his memory I need. To it I will attach the word treason and I will dedicate it to the execration of posterity.

(a pause)

After what you have just told me, I see that my opinion of France is correct. The race of Bourbons is in no condition to reign. Its government is good for priests, nobles and old countesses and is worth nothing to the real people. Yes, the people have been accustomed by the Revolution to count in the government. They will never return patiently to the nobility and the church. The army will never be Bourbon—our victories and our misfortunes have established between it and myself an indestructible link. With me she can regain power and glory—with the Bourbons she'll get nothing but insults and blows. Kings are sustained by fear or love and the Bourbons are neither loved nor feared. They hurl themselves at the base of the throne but they cannot maintain themselves for long. The French don't know how to conspire. I must help them. They are waiting. I have for me the people and the army for me—against me some old marquises whose pug dogs wouldn't dare to even bark at my shadow. Come on the day that I've waited for is come. The hour has struck. The dice are thrown.

(calling)

Grand Marshal.

BERTRAND

Sire!

BONAPARTE

Is my army ready?

BERTRAND

It's preparing according to your Majesty's order to pass in review at the port. You can hear the drum from here.

BONAPARTE

(giving him little)

Mr. Marshal have you said goodbye to your wife.

BERTRAND

Why, sire? You are not sending me away, I hope?

BONAPARTE

No, I am going to take you—

BERTRAND

May I know?

BONAPARTE

In a minute.

(Soldiers arrive to music—which plays. "Stand up, salute the Empire." Napoléon makes a sign the music stops)

Soldiers, you have left everything to follow your unhappy Emperor. Also, your Emperor loves you soldiers. I still count on you. We are going to make a last campaign. For a month the brig, the Inconstant, and these other vessels have been prepared by my orders—armed for war and provisioned for eight days. My 400 grenadiers will go in the brig with me. The two hundred Chasseurs and 100 Polish light horses will cross on the other vessels. Soldiers! I have only one word to say to you. We are going to France. We are going to Paris.

SOLDIERS

To France! To Paris! Long live France! Long live the Emperor!

LORRAIN

Sacred Rascal! I'm choking.

(The sound of a cannon)

BONAPARTE

There's the signal for departure. Friends, the first land we will see will be the soil of France. To your ranks—Grenadiers! Forward March!

(Music starts - Ca Ira - while the army marches)

LORRAIN

Well—has he forgotten me? Am I sacrificed on a desert isle?

SPY

Come on—I will do your watch. It's I who am forgotten.

(The army gets into boats)

BLACKOUT

ACT V

Tableau 18

A salon in the Faubourg St. Germain.

VALET

(opening the door of the salon)

Madame La Marquise de la Feuillade is served.

LA MARQUISE

How much I must thank Madame La Baronne de Corbelle for having procured me the pleasure of receiving you, sir! And to have been willing to accept this little family dinner.

LABREDÈCHE

I was far from expecting it, Madame la Marquise, when I met monsieur, the other day at His Excellency's—that I would have the pleasure of finding myself with him at the table of his respectable relatives.

(reading the tickets)

The Chevalier de Labredèche.

LA MARQUISE

Madame LaBaronne not being able to tell me your precise title, I took a chance on Chevalier.

LABREDÈCHE

It isn't precisely mine. Something better—But I love this title.
It's the one I had when my unfortunate father—besides "Chevalier" has something light, gallant—French even—They say "The
Chevalier de Larzun"—"The Chevalier de—de—" Well, we
have so many Chevaliers.

LA MARQUISE

And M. Le Chevalier hopes to obtain what he solicits?

LABREDÈCHE

Oh, without doubt! I am a victim of the old regime.

GRANDPARENT

By the way, you know Marquise. He wasn't named Napoléon.
The have discovered that.

ALL

What was his name then?

GRANDPARENT

His name was Nicholas.

LABREDÈCHE

Truly?

GRANDPARENT

Word of a gentleman. It's in today's journal. He's named Nicholas.

LABREDÈCHE

Nicholas, Nicholas, what a plebeian name.

ABBÉ

It's the name of a great saint.

LABREDÈCHE

Well, he has usurped the name of your great saint. This man respected nothing.

ABBÉ

Nothing! That's the word. He decreed the liberty of cults. He had no respect for medicine.

LABREDÈCHE

He ate in only ten minutes. Well—what an unnatural fellow. I said then that the minister who had great kindness for me, being assured that my family lost everything in the Revolution, that my father was executed by firing squad—and that I myself had taken an active part in the war of La Vendée—

LA MARQUISE

Ah, Chevalier, you were in La Vendée?

LABREDÈCHE

Yes, madam, at the famous battle of Torfou where Kléber and his 30,000 Mayençais were beaten by us. Not one would have remained, madam, if Kléber hadn't called one of his aides de camp named Schevarden and said to him, "Schevarden, take 200 men and go kill them at the Roussay Bridge. You will save the Army." Really—what despotism.

GRANDPARENT

By God! If he had ordered me to do that, I would have replied, "I don't take orders from a republican, from a blue, from a brigand, from a commoner like you."

LABREDÈCHE

Well, he didn't dare to respond to him like that.

LA MARQUISE

And.

LABREDÈCHE

He replied, "Yes, general" and killed them.

GRANDPARENT

The coward.

LABREDÈCHE

I said that the minister, seeing my rights, has sent me to the Army. So I am going to profit by the first chance to put before His Majesty's eyes the scene of the losses I have suffered. But I haven't figured out how to get to the pavilion at Marson. I haven't yet been able to obtain entrance to the Court.

LA MARQUISE

But here's my brother, who is the Grand Master of the Dressing Room and who will—

LITTLE COUSIN

(a girl)

Auntie, isn't the grand Master of the Dressing Room the one who—?

LA MARQUISE

Shhh! Child! When you are getting married, you don't speak of things like that.

LABREDÈCHE

Miss is going to marry—and who is the happy mortal?

LA MARQUISE

It's my son. A marriage of convenience—of fortune. The little one, just as you see her, has twenty-nine quarters.

LABREDÈCHE

And the Marquis?

LA MARQUISE

Thirty-one.

LABREDÈCHE

But that's very nice! For a total of sixty—I still have only….

GRANDPARENT

But Monsieur Le Chevalier, the name Labredèche is very well known. I still know my Hozier by heart.

LABREDÈCHE

It's a Vendean name.

GRANDPARENT

There's a Labredèche in the Vendean nobility?

LABREDÈCHE

Déche, déche, déche.

GRANDPARENT

Ah, I recall it, sir, but it seems to me, that the usurper had accorded—

LABREDÈCHE

Yes, it's true. He branded me with a pension of 1,200 francs. I refused it—but he threatened to execute me, you understand. It's around the same time, Monsieur Le Baron that he imposed the title of Count on you.

GRANDPARENT

Yes, yes, how happily he is fallen—the despot!

LABREDÈCHE

Yes, happily.

GRANDPARENT

I have lost my title.

LABREDÈCHE

And I, my pension.

GRANDPARENT

But I am reclaiming my title.

LABREDÈCHE

And I, my pension.

GRANDPARENT

We will get them, my friend, we will get them.

LABREDÈCHE

(aside)

He called me his friend, a man who sees the king face to face everyday.

(with enthusiasm)

Ah, Grand Master, yes, the good times are returning. First Colonel, I hope there'll be no more fighting this winter and that you don't take quarters until September of October—right into

Spring. As for those of us who have emigrated—for I emigrated, Madame, one of the first to do it, they will return our wealth from the plunderers.

ABBÉ

And those of the clergy, I hope.

LABREDÈCHE

But of course, each priest will return to his rights of vassalage.

LITTLE COUSIN

Auntie, what is the right of vassalage?

LA MARQUISE

Hush, little one! You ask the most inconvenient questions.

LABREDÈCHE

Each priest will have a thousand peasants, each curé his deme, the smallest Abbé his six thousands francs of rent just for sleeping double if he snores.

GRANDPARENT

Ah! Sir, this time is still far off.

LABREDÈCHE

We will get there, sir, we will get there—look at the journals— estimable papers! Little by little, they heap encroachments on the Revolution. The titus begins to be in bad tone. The pigeon wing gains favor and the queue imperceptibly—as for those ladies— they've always been of the opposition—they won't stop wearing rouge.

LA MARQUISE

(rising)

Gentlemen, will you go to the salon—coffee is waiting for us.

LABREDÈCHE

Madame La Marquise.

LA MARQUISE

My little cousin.

GRANDPARENT

My dear sister.

LA MARQUISE

Abbé, carry Cocotte.

(The Abbé takes the parakeet on his stick and marches)

BLACKOUT

ACT V

Tableau 19

Aboard the Inconstant—*the bridge.*

BONAPARTE

Grand Marshal.

BERTRAND

Sire?

BONAPARTE

I gave you, before leaving Elba, a secret package.

BERTRAND

Here it is.

BONAPARTE

It contains two proclamations which I have drawn up in advance. Work with my secretary and make copies.

(The Secretary and Bertrand seat themselves.)

LORRAIN

(pushing his head through a hatchway)

Pardon sire, excuse me, sire—it's only two words.

BONAPARTE

Speak, my brave.

LORRAIN

You see, sire—we are 400, in the hold which can't hold 150. That makes it a little uncomfortable.

BONAPARTE

Courage, my braves. The crossing won't last much longer.

LORRAIN

When I say a little, it's a manner of speaking. We're really in bad shape. I figured a way—for one to lie on top of the other but no one wants to be underneath.

BONAPARTE

Well.

LORRAIN

Well, they ask to take a little air on the bridge 'cause they are suffocating. Oh, word of honor, it's stifling in there.

BONAPARTE

(aside)

Poor men.

(aloud)

My friends, it is important that this ship be taken for a merchant boat, and that will be impossible if they are on the bridge. But if some of you come out for a bit, then to be succeeded by others—

ALL

Long live the Emperor!

(They leave.)

A SAILOR

(in the mast)

A sail! A sail!

BONAPARTE

It is coming on us?

SAILOR

From the rear.

BONAPARTE

What is it?

SAILOR

A brig!

BONAPARTE

Armed for war?

SAILOR

Yes.

BONAPARTE

What flag?

SAILOR

French.

BONAPARTE

Do you know it?

SAILOR

It's the *Zephyr*—Captain Andrieux.

BONAPARTE

Cannoneers to your guns!

(to soldiers)

All on the bridge. Each sleep with his musket on the side of him and be ready. If they don't attack as we will let them pass. If they attack us we will take them. Ah—ah—they see us. True—God it comes on us like a race horse. Thirty-six guns at the ready and we have only twenty-four.

(to Captain)

Captain, what do you say?

INCONSTANT CAPTAIN

Your Majesty commands here.

BONAPARTE

Here I am a naval officer. So be it. Give me your speakway trumpet. Silence children. Here's the one who's speaking to us.

(The brig Zephyr *crosses the* Inconstant. *The Captain is on the bridge with a megaphone.)*

ZEPHYR CAPTAIN

Hey! For what port are you sailing?

BONAPARTE

Golfe-Juan.

ZEPHYR CAPTAIN

Where do you come from?

BONAPARTE

The Isle of Elba.

ZEPHYR CAPTAIN

How's the Emperor?

BONAPARTE

Fine.

ZEPHYR CAPTAIN

Bon Voyage.

BONAPARTE

(handing the megaphone back to the Captain)

Thanks. Well, Mr. Grand Marshal, where are you in your proclamation?

BERTRAND

Sire, it's impossible to read it.

BONAPARTE

Give it to me.

(trying to read)

Cursed writing.

(crumpling it in his hand and throwing it into the sea).

Write:

Proclamation of his Majesty, the Emperor, to the Army in the Gulf of Juan. March 1, 1815. Napoléon, by the Constitution of the Empire, Emperor of the French, and King of Italy.

(Dictating)

Soldiers!

We were not vanquished. Two men left our ranks, betraying their laurels, their country, their benefactor. Soldiers, in my exile, I have heard your voices. I have come despite all obstacles and perils. Your general, called to the throne by the choice of the people, and raised on your shields, comes to you. Join him. Tear off the colors the nation has proscribed and which for twenty-six years served to rally the enemies of France. Hoist the Tricolor cockade you wore on your great journeys. We must forget we have been the masters of nations but we must not suffer them to meddle in our affairs.

Who pretends to be our master? Who has the power? You took their Eagles at Ulm, at Austerlitz, at Jena, and Eylan, at Friedland, at Tudela, at Eckmuhl, at Essling, at Wagram, at Smolensk at Moscow at Lutzen at Montmirail. Do you think that this handful of arrogant Bourbons can stand to face them? They will return to where they came from, and if they like they can reign as they pretend to have reigned for the last nineteen years.

Soldiers, come range yourself under the flags of your chief. His existence is no different from yours, his interest; his honor, his glory are not otherwise then your interests your honor, your glory. Victory and the imperial Eagles will march to the national colors and fly higher and higher to the towers or Notre Dame.

In your old age, surrounded and honored by citizens, they will ask you with respect to recount your high deeds—you can say with pride, "and I too." I took part in the Grand Army which twice entered the walls of Vienna, Rome, Berlin, Madrid and Moscow, which delivered Paris from the stain and the treason that the presence of the enemy had imprinted on it.

Honor to these brave soldiers, the glory of the country, and eternal shame to those French criminals who fought for twenty-five years with foreigners to tear the heart out of the fatherland.

Signed: Napoléon.

LORRAIN

Yes! My word of honor it is fine! I had tears in my eyes. And yet I only cried once in my life when I left my poor mother. Good woman—

A SAILOR

(in the masts)

Land.

ANOTHER SAILOR

Land.

BONAPARTE

On your knees children—and you gentlemen, say if it is France.

(a moment of solemn silence)

And now there's no reason to hide. Raise the Tricolor and salute it with a cannon.

ALL THE SOLDIERS

(placing their caps on the point of their bayonets)

Long live France!

BONAPARTE

(to a General)

Take ten men, two officers, go to reconnoiter the coast with the Caroline. Well, yes, my friends, its our France, our dear France. We are going to see it again. Our Paris, so beautiful with the bridges of Austerlitz and Jena, its Pantheon and its Column.

LORRAIN

Sacred Rascal! Sire, do you think those rogues of Cossacks have carried all of this off for their museum of Curiosities—especially my column.

BONAPARTE

No, my friend, be easy. Besides, if they've beaten it down, we will recapture enough of their cannon to make another. To the coast! To the coast!

(Everybody gets in landing boats. Napoléon puts his foot on the soil of France.)

BONAPARTE

Welcome, sacred soil! France—well loved! God is my witness that I would never set foot on your shore if I didn't believe that I did it for the good of your sons and of the world.

Mr. Grand Marshal let these men approach. They are my children. Come friend, it's me—your Emperor. Your father, your Napoléon.

PEASANT

(falling to his knees)

Sire, I am an old soldier. I didn't believe I'd ever see you again. I cannot leave you again.

BONAPARTE

Well—you see him Bertrand. Already we have reinforcements. Children—we've landed in the midst of a wood of olives—it's a good augury. Lorrain, your musket. This is the only musket shot that will be fired from here to Paris. March, my boys, to Paris.

ALL

To Paris! To Paris!

BLACKOUT

ACT V

Tableau 20

The Guard Hall at the Tuileries.

AIDE DE CAMP

Prepare relays all along the route. Here's a pass-port. Don't wait an instant. What news, gentlemen?

FIRST GUARD

You know it better than we do. They say Monsieur came here accompanied by a single gendarme.

AIDE DE CAMP

It's true! But Marshal Ney?

SECOND GUARD

What! Don't you know?

FIRST GUARD

What?

SECOND GUARD

He's been abandoned by all his soldiers and forced to join Bonaparte.

FIRST GUARD

The mayors and all the municipal officers are rushing to meet him and if they refuse to admit him the people break the gates and place the keys at his feet.

SECOND GUARD

Ah, gentlemen.

(Enter the Marquis de la Feuillade, and Labredèche.)

MARQUIS

Good day my friends.

ALL

New? Any news?

MARQUIS

Well, the Emperor is coming at a gallop.

FIRST GUARD

Where is he?—a little closer.

MARQUIS

They know it! This man comes like the wind.

AIDE DE CAMP

Colonel, the King wishes to see you. Come in.

MARQUIS

Goodbye.

AIDE DE CAMP

Gentlemen, you will not leave your uniforms. It is possible that you must take horse from one moment to the next.

SECOND GUARD

Ah, Regnier's coming.

(at the window)

What news?

VOICE

(in the street)

They say the Emperor was nearly assassinated, but the assassin was arrested.

SECOND GUARD

It's an infamy to have put a price on his head like a mad dog.

FIRST GUARD

All ways are good to get rid of such a dangerous man.

SECOND GUARD

That means you would assassinate him?

FIRST GUARD

My word, I believe I'd prefer to be an assassin than a traitor.

SECOND GUARD

The gentlemen will do me the honor of giving me satisfaction.

FIRST GUARD

Sire, you know we cannot leave.

SECOND GUARD

Well, here then.

OTHER GUARDS

In this place, gentlemen, when the King has need of us?

FIRST GUARD

Where are you running, Mr. Guard Master?

GUARD MASTER

To carry an order from the King. Gentlemen, you will serve as escort.

(to his domestic)

Run to my home and prepare my old robe of Senator. I will try to be there in an hour. Reassure my wife. Tell her I won't compromise myself—and for her to be easy.

(great noise outside)

What's that?

THIRD GUARD

A mob rally.

FIRST GUARD

Ah! Regnier, what's going on?

VOICE

(in this street)

A man was just stopped with the tricolor flag.

LABREDÈCHE

(in the street)

It's I, it's I who stopped him.

ALL THE GUARDS

Good my brave, good—

VALET

(crossing)

The carriage of Madam, the Duchess of Angoulème.

ALL THE GUARDS

What's this?

LABREDÈCHE

(entering with a tricolor flag)

Here I am. My trophy.

FIRST GUARD

Is Madam leaving?

LABREDÈCHE

Is all the world out there? I was nearly shot while crossing the Marsau pavilion. Let it alone, let it alone. I took this flag at the risk of my life, I won't lose it.

(aside)

It may be useful. They say the other fellow is at Fontainebleau.

CAPTAIN

(entering)

A horse, gentlemen, a horse.

(All the Guards leave)

VALET

The carriages of the Comte d'Artois are ready.

AIDE DE CAMP

Imbecile! Where are you going, sir? Mr. Introducer of Ambassa-dors!

INTRODUCER

Make my excuses to the King. I learned that my wife has just had a baby.

(aside)

If the Emperor would only consent to be godfather.

LABREDÈCHE

(after having put his flag behind some furniture.)

Ah, Monsieur, Master of the Wardrobe—a moment? You are not going like this? My petition! My petition! Ah! I wanted to see what you thought. You were betrayed before me. It's a trap that is set for you. And you call a brigand, an ogre, Napoléon, the Great, Emperor of the French and King of Italy, Protector of the Confederation of the Rhine, mediator of the Swiss Federation! My petition.

MASTER

Sir, it's impossible. I put it before the eyes of the King and His Majesty having regard to your services, and the misfortunes of your family has granted you a pension of 1,200 francs.

LABREDÈCHE

A pension of 1,200 francs?

GUARD MASTER

It is inscribed in the Great Book since yesterday and here is the seal.

LABREDÈCHE

The seal is registered.

(aside)

…and the other one will be here in a half hour.

(aloud)

Well, it won't ruin your king, such graces don't cost much. He grants it today and he leaves tomorrow. His pension will have been paid to me for one day. 1,200 francs a year—it's three pounds ten sous to which I am entitled. I have nothing against the Bourbon family. I am a disinterested man. I love and admire the Emperor, do you hear? I tear up your seal.

(aside)

Don't throw the pieces away, they may be useful.

(aloud)

Know sir, that I have had two brothers frozen in Russia.

(aside)

I believe the time has come to replace my brothers.

AIDE DE CAMP

Sentry, don't let anybody leave.

LABREDÈCHE

Well, here I am shut in? Compromised with the Royal Family.

(to the Courtiers)

This is an indignity, gentlemen.

SENTINEL

Gentlemen, no one can leave.

SEVERAL VOICES

What? Why?

COURTIER

But I will be compromised if the Emperor finds me here.

A SECOND COURTIER

If I had at least been able to change these clothes.

LABREDÈCHE

Monsieur, Le Comte

(aside)

Devil, he has decorations and stars worth 1,200 francs at least—a year of my pension.

(aloud)

Monsieur Le Comte, if you wish, sire, you can mix in the crowd without being recognized.

COUNT

Oh, my friend, what a service!

(they change clothes.)

There! My hat—give me yours—I must sacrifice.

SOME VOICES

It's the King who's losing everything of ours.

OTHER VOICES

No, it's the Chamber.

OTHERS

If the King had not proposed the laws.

MARQUIS

(reentering)

The King will pass this way, gentlemen. Silence, whatever your opinions. Royalists—don't forget that he is the son of Saint Louis. Liberals, remember that it is to him you owe the Charter. Respect to misfortune and gray hair.

(Louis XVIII passes through. Profound silence. Courtiers follow him and speak in leaving).

FIRST COURTIER

Are you going to Gand?

SECOND COURTIER

No.

THIRD COURTIER

And the Vicomte?

FOURTH COURTIER

I accompany His Majesty.

FIFTH COURTIER

And I stay here. It's necessary to speak to the Emperor.

LABREDÈCHE

(pulling from his pocket a tricolor cockade)

Let's put on the national colors. Now the other fellow can come.

ONE OF THE REMAINING COURTIERS

Oh, sir, where did you get this cockade? If I could only have one.

SECOND COURTIER

And I.

THIRD COURTIER

Me, too.

FOURTH COURTIER

You're not selling it, perhaps?

LABREDÈCHE

I have some, gentlemen. I have enough for us all. I've conspired for a long while. I had correspondence with Elba. I've known for three months that our Emperor would return. What a man!

ANOTHER

And they called him a tyrant.

LABREDÈCHE

Him, a tyrant! He was good—to have given me a pension because my two brothers were frozen to death in Russia.

(aside)

This is not the moment to speak of my father.

SEVERAL PEOPLE

(coming in)

The Emperor has just entered Paris.

LABREDÈCHE

(to an Usher)

My friend, here's five francs. Run to my house, 50 Rue de la Harpe, tell them to put my four lamps out—a holiday by God. Long live the Emperor!

CRIES IN THE DISTANCE

Ah, ah. He's here. He's here!

LABREDÈCHE

Do you hear, gentlemen? He's here—the conqueror of the world approaches—we are going to see him face to face.

ANOTHER

What joy!

CRIES APPROACHING

Long live the Emperor! Long live the Emperor!

(Some general officers enter)

LABREDÈCHE

Be welcome, gentlemen. We are waiting on you. We are waiting on the Emperor.

OFFICER

He's following us, gentlemen.

VOICE

(outside)

Here he is. Long live the Emperor! Sire—no, we will carry you. It's in our arms that Your Majesty must reenter his palace.

BONAPARTE

(entering)

Yes, my boys, yes I thank you. Yes, I am your father, your Emperor. Your joy goes to my heart. My friends, you know when the Emperor returns to the Tuileries, the flag is returned.

VOICES

A flag! A flag!

LABREDÈCHE

What a piece of luck!

(aloud)

A flag! I have one, a flag that I brought here in the midst of a thousand dangers and that I hid for eight months for this memorable day. Here it is, sire—I am happy to be the first to offer to Your Majesty the proof of devotion to his august person.

SEVERAL VOICES

Raise it! Raise it!

BONAPARTE

I've seen you before.

LABREDÈCHE

Sire, Your Majesty granted me a pension of 1,200 francs.

COURTIERS

Your Majesty wishes to receive our congratulations.

ALL

Sire—Your Majesty.

BONAPARTE

Yes, gentlemen, but don't forget it is a revolution of soldiers and NCOs. There's many profit, perhaps, but it is the people who have done it—it's to them I owe everything.

USHER

Sire, the Envoys from the Chamber of Deputies are here.

BONAPARTE

Bring them in.

ANOTHER USHER

The Envoys from the Chamber of Peers.

BONAPARTE

Gentlemen, envoys of the Chamber of Deputies. The Chamber is rendered unworthy of the confidence of the nation in making the people pay expenses spent by foreigners for spilling French blood. I abolish the Chamber of Deputies.

Gentlemen, envoys of the Chamber of Peers, the Chamber is composed in part of men who bore arms against their country. They have an interest in reestablishing feudal rights and in the annulment of national rights. I dismiss the Chamber of Peers. I will call electors to the camp in May and there I will consecrate the rights of the people—for the throne is made for the nation and the nation for the throne. I hope for peace—I don't fear war—My Eagles always have their wings spread. And my slogan is the gallant: "Do what I must, come what may."

ALL

Long live the Emperor!

BERTRAND

Sire, you are greater than ever!

BONAPARTE

Then I do not regret one day of Elba.

CURTAIN

ACT VI

Tableau 21

St. Helena, 1821. The valley of James Town. Napoléon's point of view. Roadstead passing over the long chain of mountains opposite Longwood and facing the Plantation House. The road, large at first and bifurcated recedes into the distance and disappears, at its point of junction on the plain inclined to the coast, at the foot of which some edifices can be seen. It's the city of Jamestown at the edge of which one discovers the sea. The scene is encased at right and left by rocky escarpments where the two branches of the road disappear and sink. The one to the right of the spectator leads to Longwood, and the other to his left leads to Nylass.

(Napoléon is on the peak of a rock facing the ocean.)

SIR HUDSON LOWE

(at the front, speaking to an NCO)

If General Bonaparte wishes to ride by horse today, as I have received new orders from my government, you will accompany him at ten paces distance, never further.

NCO

Yes, Sir Hudson Lowe.

(Napoléon, pensive, descends the rock and goes out slowly by the left)

Recall, sir, that any attempt to assist in the escape of the general will be punished by death. I mention this because you've only been here for a month.

NCO

Yes, sir.

(Hudson Lowe leaves. Santini appears from the opposite side, aims at the governor then seeing the NCO lowers his musket.)

SANTINI

Demon English!

(approaches singing)

But you know how you rule over me?

NCO

(who saw him aim at Sir Hudson Lowe)

Ah—you hunt, sir?

SANTINI

Yes, the Emperor is poorly nourished. So I want to add something for dinner.

NCO

What are you hunting?

SANTINI

Two little birds. Larks.

NCO

Yes! Yes! Some larks. You have a pretty musket.

SANTINI

It's a French musket.

NCO

Show it.

SANTINI

Why?

NCO

I want to see how well it sights. I'd like to be a hunter, too.

SANTINI

Ah! Ah!

NCO

Yes! Yes!

(aiming)

Good.

(he fires at the trunk of a tree. The ball makes it jump. He goes to the tree and with a knife retrieves the ball, then returns to Santini)

Is this the little plum with which you are hunting larks? You shoot well, friend, if you kill birds with that.

SANTINI

What do you mean to say?

NCO

For whom was this ball?

SANTINI

For the governor—and to rest for me.

NCO

To kill the governor?

SANTINI

Aren't you English?

NCO

Imbecile.

SANTINI

Why are you here?

NCO

To save the Emperor.

SANTINI

Your plans?

NCO

He knows them.

SANTINI

He entrusts it to you?

NCO

Yes.

SANTINI

He knows you then?

NCO

Yes.

SANTINI

For how long?

NCO

Before you ever heard of his name.

SANTINI

I have served him for seven years.

NCO

And I for thirty, do you understand?

SANTINI

And how will you speak to him?

NCO

I will accompany him on horseback.

SANTINI

He doesn't wish to ride.

NCO

Then I will enter.

SANTINI

He doesn't receive English officers.

NCO

You will tell him I have the password.

SANTINI

He doesn't give any.

NCO

He's given me one.

SANTINI

What is it?

NCO

Toulon and Liberty.

SANTINI

You are French.

NCO

As truly as you are Corsican.

SANTINI

What's your family?

CAPTAIN

I haven't any.

SANTINI

Are you a soldier?

SPY

No.

SANTINI

But who are you?

SPY

A spy. Go.

SANTINI

Goodbye.

SPY

Au revoir.

BLACKOUT

ACT VI

Tableau 22

LAS CASES

(thumbing a brochure)

What is this infamous libel?

MARCHAND

Another against the Emperor.

LAS CASES

This archbishop of malignity. This almoner of the God Mars to write to the ambassador of Varovice. Someone who hates Sir Hudson Lowe has sent it to us. Yesterday he returned the work of this English member of Parliament.

MARCHAND

Think of it. Count: it had letters of gold on the cover—"To Napoléon the Great."

LAS CASES

The address was well taken.

MARCHAND

Also, the Emperor has not received it.

LAS CASES

Shame and pity.

MARCHAND

The Emperor! The Emperor!

BONAPARTE

(entering)

You are hiding something

LAS CASES

Nothing. A new libel against Your Majesty.

BONAPARTE

Let me see, let me see, child—do you believe that I am sensitive to their pinpricks. Ah, it is this poor, Abbé. He slanders, he injures. That's what it is to lose an embassy.

LAS CASES

Sire.

BONAPARTE

Let them fire and bite the dust and gnaw the grain. When they want to be read they will be just, when they want to be handsome, they will praise me. Give me the morning Chronicle and the Statesman.

LAS CASES

The governor has suppressed them.

BONAPARTE

Ah! That's fine.

LAS CASES

Your Majesty broke off his walk today.

BONAPARTE

Yes.

(to Merchant)

Give me some, coffee.

(to Las Cases)

They've penned me up, my friends. St. Helena with its eight leagues circumference is too vast, for me who traveled straight in Europe! or rather the mountain air is too pure. I need my unhealthy valley. They measure out space for me and an English soldier hides in wait when I approach the limits. How can I approach the limits? How can the sovereigns of Europe let sovereignty itself be polluted in my person? Don't they see that they are destroying themselves with their own hands at St. Helena? Really, I don't complain for myself. My complaints are for my dignity and my character—I order myself to shut up.

LAS CASES

The world will avenge you, sire. And you are more great here than at the Tuileries.

BONAPARTE

I know it well, and that makes me overlook many things. But it's at this price one becomes a figure in History. At least Regulus only suffered three days.

MARCHAND

Here's your coffee, sir. And there is the medicine from Sir Hudson Lowe.

BONAPARTE

And why medicine from Sir Hudson Lowe?

MARCHAND

The Governor has learned that Your Majesty was suffering.

BONAPARTE

He sent it to me? His doctor?

(He smells the coffee and throws it)

MARCHAND

Is the coffee bad, sir?

BONAPARTE

No, but Corvisart always forbade me coffee which smells of garlic. It still seems to me that some coffee would make me better but I haven't yet had any good coffee since I've been here and I've been better for three days. Marchand, you must get us some at whatever the price.

MARCHAND

Sire, we don't have any money.

BONAPARTE

You will barter for it with a jewel of mine.

(Noise outside)

Oh, well, what the matter? What is this noise? It's the voice of Santini. Let's see.

SIR HUDSON LOWE

(in the corridor)

French dog!

SANTINI

(in Italian)

Birbone!

BONAPARTE

Oh! A dispute between Santini and the governor.

MARCHAND

(at the door)

No one can come in.

SIR HUDSON LOWE

I must speak to him.

BONAPARTE

Let him in. Let him in. I hear you, Sir Hudson. But speak from the door. It's there I speak to my valets.

SIR HUDSON LOWE

General Bonaparte.

BONAPARTE

First of all, I am not General Bonaparte, I am the Emperor Napoléon. Address me by my title or don't address me at all.

SIR HUDSON LOWE

I have received an order from my government to only call you—

BONAPARTE

Ah, yes, from Lord Castlereagh, from Lord Bathhurst. Let them call me as they wish, they cannot prevent me from being who I am. All of them, and you who speak to me, will die forgotten, before the blood has time to leave your cadavers or if you are remembered it will be for the indignities you have heaped on me, while the Emperor Napoléon will always be the star of civilized people! Go ahead, speak. What did you want?

SIR HUDSON LOWE

That the Corsican Santini be placed in my hand.

BONAPARTE

And what has the Corsican Santini done?

SIR HUDSON LOWE

He struck one of the English soldiers who were cutting down the trees on the way to Plantation House.

LAS CASES

And why were they cutting the trees?

BONAPARTE

Why, my poor Las Cases? Why? So that the Emperor Napoléon who loves to lie in the shade will boil under their tropical sun. If they could redden the earth, the would do it.

SIR HUDSON LOWE

The government is ignorant of—

BONAPARTE

You are not ignorant of it! You have seen me seated twenty times under this shadow which recalls to me the state of Europe.

SIR HUDSON LOWE

Others will be planted.

BONAPARTE

Curse! Misfortune! And what do you wish to do with Santini?

SIR HUDSON LOWE

Send him back to France.

BONAPARTE

Oh, I will give you him with good heart. Only I insist on saying goodbye to him. You can search him when he leaves. If that's all you have to say to me, go!

SIR HUDSON LOWE

I have received orders from my government to cut down the expenses of your food.

BONAPARTE

I didn't think it was possible. And what do they give me?

SIR HUDSON LOWE

On a daily basis, you can have only one table for four people, a bottle of wine per person and invited guests once a week.

BONAPARTE

Fine! You can cut it down further. And if I'm hungry, I am going to sit myself at the table for fifty-three. These are braves. They have received the Baptism of Fire. They don't repulse the oldest soldiers of Europe. Is that all?

SIR HUDSON LOWE

I ask you why you've refused to receive my doctor. Yours may die or return to France. Then who will look after your health?

BONAPARTE

I have refused your doctor because he is yours and because we believe you capable of anything—do you understand—of anything. And so long as you nourish your hate, we will nourish our thoughts.

SIR HUDSON LOWE

You are wrong. I, who have demanded and a palace and furniture England for you from….

BONAPARTE

I have no need for a palace or furniture. Nor do I ask for an executioner or a shroud. Marchand, my boots. I am going.

MARCHAND

Here they are, sire.

BONAPARTE

Are these boots new?

MARCHAND

Yes.

BONAPARTE

Where did you get them?

MARCHAND

Sire?

BONAPARTE

Where did you get them? I hope that you were not so weak as to ask them from this governor?

MARCHAND

No sire—no. But for along while, without telling Your Majesty, I tried, I tested finally, I had them made.

BONAPARTE

My friend.

(shaking his hand)

See this, Sir Hudson Lowe—and report it to your government.

SIR HUDSON LOWE

You've decided to go horseback riding?

BONAPARTE

Yes.

SIR HUDSON LOWE

I am going to give the order for an NCO to serve as your escort.

BONAPARTE

So, I'm to have a mounted jailer. Take off my boots, Merchant. I won't ride. I'll take a bath.

SIR HUDSON LOWE

You've already taken one this morning. Water is scarce on this island.

BONAPARTE

(after a pause)

Write Las Cases.

(to Sir Hudson Lowe)

The shame of the English government is not to have sent me to St. Helena but to have given the command to Sir Hudson Lowe. So for him—counting from today, I vow his name to the execration of mankind. And when one wishes to speak of something a bit more than a jailer, and a bit less than a hangman—one will say—Sir Hudson Lowe.

(he violently shuts the door in the face of the governor)

Ah, I sense that I appear like a hurricane and I don't wish to compromise my rage with that man. Ah, well, when you complain of the brave Admiral George Cockburn! That was a man— a little thick, a little blunt, a little sharp—but this one—Lowe, his scourge greater than all the miseries of this horrid rock.

LAS CASES

Sire, you can still go out. Doctor O'Meara has prescribed exercise on horseback for you.

BONAPARTE

Yes, yes, I know that I need it. But how do you think I'll feel after a trot limited like a merry go 'round—I who used to go fifteen or twenty leagues on horseback everyday. My enemies called me the "hundred miles man"

(to Las Cases)

Here, Las Cases—here are the spurs that I brought from Dresden to Champ-Aubert. I give them to you my friend. Keep them. I will never again ride horseback.

LAS CASES

(on his knees)

Your Majesty makes me a knight without my deserving it.

BONAPARTE

Take them my friend. It's a monument and you are curious about monuments. You should have seen me when I had the swords of Frances I and Frederick the Great.

LAS CASES

It seems to me that in Your Majesty's place I would have worn one or the other.

BONAPARTE

Neither! I had my own.

LAS CASES

May Your Majesty pardon me, I am stupid sometimes.

(Enter Santini.)

BONAPARTE

Ah, it's you Santini.

(gaily)

What, pirate, you permit yourself to beat an English soldier—and that because he cut down a tree at whose foot I enjoyed sleeping—it is true?

SANTINI

Sire, outraged by the governor's cruel treatments—

BONAPARTE

He admits it! You see the wretch admits it.

SANTINI

Ah—if they hadn't snatched my musket.

BONAPARTE

Well.

SANTINI

I would have shot that dog of an Englishmen.

BONAPARTE

Well, let such an idea come to you and you would see how I will treat you. Gentlemen, here's Santini, who wants to kill the Governor! He'll get me into a fine mess. Villain!

(searching for a word)

Corsican!

SANTINI

Yes, it followed that the island must be relieved of the governor or of me. Misfortune dictates that it is I who leave! I who wanted to die for Your Majesty.

BONAPARTE

Yes, it's true, you're leaving Santini.

SANTINI

Ah, if Your Majesty would permit it. I would stay despite them. They'd have to ship me out in little pieces.

BONAPARTE

Not at all! There's no visit as regrettable as St. Helena. Hurry to leave while you can. As for me, they are going to kill me here, it's certain.

SANTINI

Your Majesty left Elba, too.

BONAPARTE

St. Helen will keep me. Go my friend, leave. The air of the sea is pure, the ocean immense. It ought to be sweet to breathe the air of the sea and to be rocked by the waves of the Ocean. In a few days you will see this torrid sun replaced by one with cloud.

(going to window)

Oh, clouds, clouds.

SANTINI

Sire, haven't you any message, any letter to give me—? I return to France.

BONAPARTE

No. They would take it from you. Only, if your destiny conducts you to Vienna try to see my son, my poor child. Say to him: "I left your father dying, exiled from the world, thrown on a rock in the midst of the ocean. Of all the wealth he has lost, he regrets only you. It's to you, he calls when he speaks alone, you he names when he dreams at night. The only portraits which decorate his chamber are yours. And when he dies, he will have your bust brought in and die with his eyes fixed on it." That's what you will say to my son, Santini. You can add that I embraced you when we parted.

SANTINI

(embracing the Emperor)

Sire, you will see him again.

BONAPARTE

How?

SANTINI

There's an English officer in the antechamber. You must see him.

BONAPARTE

Never.

SANTINI

He told me to repeat two words to you: Toulon and Liberty.

BONAPARTE

(trembling)

It is well. I will speak to him. And now my friend, have you enough money?

SANTINI

No, sire, but what does it matter?

BONAPARTE

Have you some jewels?

SANTINI

I've been obliged to sell all that I had since I came here.

BONAPARTE

(feeling his pockets)

Marchand, bring me some hidden money.

SANTINI

Why, sire?

BONAPARTE

Fine. Break them open now. They will take them from him saying he stole it from me.

(writing some words)

Take this my friend. Take this paper, too.

SANTINI

A pension, sire!

BONAPARTE

Now, adieu! Leave me. Don't forget my son. Adieu. Follow him gentlemen and send me the English officer in the antechamber.

(they leave crying. The spy enters)

Ah, it's you. I am surprised not to have seen you sooner.

SPY

Thanks—this word is already a recompense. I was not able, Sire, when the Congress deported you in 1815, I had thought to accompany you. They wouldn't have me on the *Bellerophon*. They wouldn't have me on the *Northumberland*, I offered to be a soldier, sailor, valet. They refused me, but since 1815 there has not passed one day, one hour, one minute which I was not tormented by this thought of your escape. I got myself naturalized as an Englishman. I enlisted. I passed from the Isle of France to the Indies. Then one day I embarked for St. Helena, and after a month I am near you—without your being able to doubt that in this Redcoat uniform beats a heart devoted to the Emperor and to France.

BONAPARTE

Well—

SPY

Sire, perhaps you have remarked a vessel at anchor in the distance whose sails seem like wings of a seagull.

BONAPARTE

Yes, and I am surprised that it always stays in the same place.

SPY

That's because it is waiting for you, Sire.

BONAPARTE

And how will I get there?

SPY

In a bark which is hidden at the extremity of the island.

BONAPARTE

And am I not accompanied by an English officer?

SPY

And am I not the officer who accompanies you?

BONAPARTE

That's true. And when I can I leave?

SPY

When you say "I wish it!" The vessel will stay there until I light a bunch of dry branches at the height of the rock. They will know then that the work has miscarried and they will leave. But time is precious, Sire. It took me five years to obtain this minute. May it not be wasted.

BONAPARTE

You are devoted to me. I know it.

(giving him his snuff box)

Take this as a remembrance.

SPY

It's gold.

BONAPARTE

It's a snuff box.

INTRODUCER

But gold.

BONAPARTE

(engraving his monogram with a stamp)

Wait, my monogram—engraved by me.

SPY

Oh—now.

BONAPARTE

Now—get on your bark and go.

SPY

Without you?

BONAPARTE

Without me.

SPY

It's you I came to find. I will not leave without you. You must return to France. I must restore you to the world. A great idea has come to me, I must accomplish it. I must deliver the Emperor Napoléon or I must die of it. In either case my name is made. It will live.

BONAPARTE

Ah—Ambition—I believed you devoted. I was deceived.

SPY

One evening at St. Cloud—my devotion which began at Toulon, ceased. You had let me live, I saved your life. We were quits, since that day I ceased to be under obligations to you—I became your enthusiast Sire. Remember at Elba you received me better and returned to France.

BONAPARTE

Well—it's because of that. I cannot do what I've already done.

SPY

Sire, you will continue your history.

BONAPARTE

And what chapter would I add? My career is full. In leaving here I risk falling—in staying I can rise again.

SPY

I understand you, and I listen at your feet. Speak! Speak!

BONAPARTE

It's this—you have understood me. Do you see it is only vulgar administration which becomes a cult. Jesus Christ had not founded a religion if he hadn't had his forty days or passion. Oh my passion, mine, my cross is St. Helena, I protect it, I need it.

SPY

Kléber is right: you are as great as the world.

BONAPARTE

For me to escape, flee! Only my death is lacking. A few days, a few hours perhaps,—that is all life remains to me. For I sense the all that one feels when one is going to die. Where will I find a tomb more imposing—if I follow your advice? St. Helen hewn like a peak—isn't it a magnificent pedestal for the colossal statue the people will one day raise for me.

SPY

But your son, your son.

BONAPARTE

Well, my name—isn't that a fine enough heritage?

SPY

Well—all is said.

BONAPARTE

Where are you going?

SPY

(leaving)

I will return.

BONAPARTE

(pensive)

This man had the instinct for good—why has he strayed from his path—

(turning around)

What is that? Fire? An incendiary?

SPY

(returning)

Nothing, I just gave the fire signal.

BONAPARTE

And the boat is going to leave?

SPY

Yes.

BONAPARTE

And you?

SPY

I stay.

BONAPARTE

Oh—misfortune. Here's the governor. What have you done?

SIR HUDSON LOWE

(at the door)

Why, this fire? Is it a signal?

SPY

Yes.

SIR HUDSON LOWE

Why?

SPY

To correspond with the ship which is at anchor in the sea.

SIR HUDSON LOWE

And what was the ship doing?

SPY

It was waiting for the Emperor if the Emperor had wished to escape.

SIR HUDSON LOWE

And the Emperor?

SPY

Doesn't wish it!

SIR HUDSON LOWE

(astonished)

Doesn't wish it!

SPY

No, you couldn't understand.

SIR HUDSON LOWE

And who made this plot?

SPY

Me.

SIR HUDSON LOWE

You, an Englishman?

SPY

(throwing his hat)

Me—a Frenchman.

SIR HUDSON LOWE

You know the price?

SPY

Yes.

SIR HUDSON LOWE

The penalty?

SPY

Yes.

SIR HUDSON LOWE

Are you ready?

SPY

Yes.

SIR HUDSON LOWE

Your trial won't be lengthy.

SPY

I know it.

SIR HUDSON LOWE

From the yardarm.

SPY

So be it! I will have the honor of a cannon.

(to Napoléon)

Adieu, sire—you understand. I am going to hang. It's a bit your fault—you could have shot me at Toulon. Adieu.

(he leaves with the governor)

BONAPARTE

Au revoir! Till we meet again. I feel my God. Ah! Ah!

(he falls on the sofa, unconscious)

MARCHAND

(at the door)

Can one come in? Sire—can one come in. The Emperor, sleeping, pale, not responding—oh, come, doctor, and see.

ANTONMARCHI

He has fainted. Carry him to his bed. The evening air will make him better.

BLACKOUT

ACT VI

Tableau 23

The Bedchamber.

MARCHAND

(knocking on the door)

Mr. Las Cases—Mr. Las Cases.

LAS CASES

Well, how's the Emperor?

MARCHAND

He's weakening, more and more. Do you know something about this French spy and why after eight days he's yet to be executed when the decree says that any Frenchman who tries to aid in the escape of the Emperor will be executed immediately?

LAS CASES

He was carrying an English NCO commission and considered as such he could only be judged by a court martial. But this won't save him. Antonmarchi has gone to town to get the news.

MARCHAND

His arrest made the Emperor more sick than a year of suffering

LAS CASES

Oh, Marchand! To see him thus weaken day by day—hour by hour and not to be able to bring help even at the price of my blood, of my life! It seems to me that Europe will say to us, "You were there, near him, and you let him die."

BERTRAND

(at the door)

The Emperor asks for his will. He wants to add some legacies.

LAS CASES

I'll bring it to him. Marchand, try to learn where it is in French procedure. I would give ten years of my life to learn that the Emperor is saved.

MARCHAND

(following him to the door)

Oh, if the Emperor is worse, call me. His Will—He fears he's forgotten someone. The world which slanders him will know he was good.

ENGLISH SOLDIER

A letter from the governor for General Bonaparte.

MARCHAND

Good. Ought I to show it to him? Perhaps it contains some news of France. It's the seal of Sir Hudson Lowe—that doesn't bode well.

BERTRAND

(at the door)

Marchand, the Emperor saw from the window an English soldier bringing a letter. He wishes to see it—

MARCHAND

Monsieur Marshal, it is from the governor. Should you take it to him?

BERTRAND

He wishes it.

(going back)

MARCHAND

Ah, here's Doctor Antonmarchi. Well what news?

ANTONMARCHI

Condemned.

MARCHAND

To death?

ANTONMARCHI

To death.

(One hears a violent ringing in the chamber)

MARCHAND

Despair! What's that?

LAS CASES

(coming in)

Antonmarchi, Antonmarchi, oh, doctor, come, come, the Emperor is in a frightful crisis. A letter which he received contained the court martial decree.

BONAPARTE

(in the corridor)

Leave me! Leave me!

ANTONMARCHI

Sire.

BONAPARTE

Go away!

LAS CASES

Ah—see—see how pale he is.

BONAPARTE

(entering)

Listen, listen all to my last legacy. And I wish the whole world was here to hear it. I leave the opprobrium of my death to the reigning house in England. And now I am finished with the world. Come, my friends, my children, I am no longer Emperor. I am a dying man who suffers—a father who blesses you. Ah—if Lorsey were here, my brave Lorsey. He could not cure me, I know it but perhaps, if he could deflect my illness to another part of my body, that would be some ease. This kills me. This gnaws me. It's like a knife whose blade was broken, buried in the flesh. Oh, this is atrocious.

(pause)

Close the window. Yes, yes, my poor Marchand, like that—Thanks. Don't let me see that burning sun anymore. It's the heavens that kill me. Oh my friends—where are the clouds of Charleroi? My child.

ANTONMARCHI

Take the Emperor to his bed.

BONAPARTE

No. I suffer too much. Take this cloak, cover me with this cloak. It will never leave me again. It's the one I wore at Marengo. Ah! My friend how much trouble I am giving you—and how bad it is to die.

ANTONMARCHI

What are you doing, Sire?

BONAPARTE

I am praying. Not everyone has the advantage of being an atheist, or a doctor, doctor. Now I want to see my son a little more. Oh, my son—my child—if he knew that his father was dying here guarded by jailers. But he knows nothing. He is happy. He plays. Poor little one. Someday he will know how I suffered—won't he? Through you my friends. Through my good Las Cases—through my memoirs if the English don't destroy them.

(pause)

Ah, my son won't bear the name of his father—ah, the Austrians, who surround him are going to inspire him with horror of me! My son is going to hate me. My God! Ah, tell me that my son won't hate me, that he won't hate his father.

(enter the governor followed by Dr. Arnott)

Oh—what's this man want of me?

LAS CASES

(to Sir Hudson Lowe)

Leave, sir, leave!

SIR HUDSON LOWE

I have orders from my government not to leave General Bonaparte from the moment there is fear of—

LAS CASES

(raising a horsewhip)

Silence!

BONAPARTE

Leave him alone—leave this man alone, Los Cases. I don't see him. I watch my son. Open the window. The evening air will make me better perhaps. The sun is setting and fading, and I too, I'm fading. Ah!—a cloud, a cloud which has passed over France, France my dear France. My child. Give me one of his pictures, one which is embroidered by Marie Louise. I can no longer see his bust, but I can still feel it in my hands—oh, if I see his pretty blond hair—but nothing. Nothing, nothing—at 2,000 leagues. Oh, my breast. They say that they torture me. Oh these kings let them come see their patient. This uniform makes me ill. My sword—give me my sword. To me—to my great battles. Marengo. Austerlitz. Jena—Waterloo! Waterloo!

(He falls on his bed. Enter Mme. Bertrand and her children—all the household).

BERTRAND

Help the Emperor, help him Monsieur Antonmarchi—don't you see he is dying?

BONAPARTE

For my son. My name—nothing but my name.

(a pause)

Head of the army. My God! My God! The French nation.

ANTONMARCHI

(putting his hand on the Emperor's heart)

The Emperor is dead.

(They kneel.)

SIR HUDSON LOWE

(drawing his watch)

Six minutes to six. Good.

(they hear a cannon shot)

DOCTOR ARNOTT

(turning)

What's that?

SIR HUDSON LOWE

Nothing: A spy has just been hanged.

CURTAIN

ABOUT FRANK J. MORLOCK

FRANK J. MORLOCK has written and translated many plays since retiring from the legal profession in 1992. His translations have also appeared on Project Gutenberg, the Alexandre Dumas Père web page, Literature in the Age of Napoléon, Infinite Artistries.com, and Munsey's (formerly Blackmask). In 2006 he received an award from the North American Jules Verne Society for his translations of Verne's plays. He lives and works in México.